The Richest Man in Persia
The Way to Safe, Ethical Wealth

Brian Morgan

This paperback edition first published for world-wide consumption by The Writers Trust, 2012.

Copyright © and Trade Marks 2012 Brian Morgan and The Writers Trust. This book is copyright under the Berne Convention. All rights reserved world-wide. No part of this publication may be stored in a retrieval system, transmitted or reproduced in any way, including, but not limited to, digital copying and printing.

The right of Brian Morgan to be identified as the author of this work has been asserted in accordance with sections 77 and 78 of the Copyright, Designs and Patents Act, 1988. Intellectual property rights have been assigned by the author to The Writers Trust.

The author, Brian Morgan, and the publisher, The Writers Trust, have made their best effort to produce a high quality, informative and helpful book. But they make no representation or warranties of any kind with regard to the completeness or accuracy of the content of the book. They accept no liability of any kind for any losses or damages caused, or alleged to be caused, directly or indirectly, from using the information contained in this book.

This book is associated with the following website: www.BrianMorganBooks.com. An eBook version of this book is available on that website.

Produced for the publisher in the United States of America by the resources of CreateSpace and available world-wide through Amazon.

ISBN: 1475177267
ISBN-13: 978-1475177268

"A big heart is a great gift to the world. Abundance comes from helping other people enrich their lives. If you have it in your heart to make life better for others, and, if you follow the Codes that are necessary to create wealth, then you will have riches beyond your dreams.
But remember, money should always be used to enhance the values that are important to you. Money should never come at the cost of virtue. A good name is better than a girdle of gold, but there is no reason why you should not have both – a good name *and* a girdle of gold."

Tragoas, the Richest Man in Persia.

Dedication

This book is dedicated to my beloved wife, Judy, who has encouraged and supported me for more than 50 years. I would be nothing without her. She is the inspiration behind the Minab of this story.

It is also dedicated to my children,
Fiona Scully and Michael Morgan,
and to Dennis Scully.

And also to my grandchildren
(in order of appearance in my life),
Sean Scully, Thomas Morgan, Bridget Scully,
Elizabeth Morgan and Mikaela Morgan.

I love them all.

Contents

Author's Note
The Fires of Fate
The Testimony of Tragoas
Code 1: The Quest for Real Riches
Code 2: Master your Mind.
Code 3: Master Time.
Code 4: Cast off your Rags.
Code 5: A World of Abundance.
Code 6: No-one Becomes Rich Alone.
Code 7: The Power of Leverage.
Code 8: Many Streams of Income.
Code 9: Investments - Magic Carpet to Riches.
Code 10: Business Secrets of the Masters
Code 11: The Special Few.
Epilogue
Your Notes
About the Author

BRIAN MORGAN

Author's Note

Millions of people around the world have read and profited by *The Richest Man in Babylon*, by George S. Clason. This book has been hailed as "the greatest of all inspirational works on the subject of thrift and personal wealth".

In 1926, George Clason, from Missouri in America, issued the first of what was to become a famous series of pamphlets on the subject of financial success. The author used parables set in ancient Babylon to make each of his easy-to-follow points. The pamphlets were distributed in large quantities by banks and insurance companies and were loved by millions of readers.

The most famous of these pamphlets was *The Richest Man in Babylon*, so this became the obvious title when a number of the parables were gathered together into a book by that name.

The Richest Man in Babylon has gone through many reprints and is still in print, and on best-seller lists, some eight decades after George Clason first set pen to paper. Millions have read it. It has become a modern inspirational classic as relevant today as it was all those years ago.

Read it. Profit by it. Then read this story, *The Richest Man in Persia*, which was inspired by George Clason's work and contains "the untold wealth secrets of Persia", as excavated from the ruins of "the wealthiest city under the sun", Persepolis, not far from Babylon in the ancient Persian Empire.

The pages that follow will give the background to the amazing discovery that could change the lives of millions, as *The Richest Man in Babylon* has done.

Brian Morgan
www.BrianMorganBooks.com.

The Fires of Fate

The background to this story of ethical wealth creation involves King Darius III and his heroic defense of the Persian Empire against the might of Alexander the Great of Macedonia. The legend has fascinated scholars and others through the centuries.

Alexander thought himself godlike, and thus invincible, and it was in this belief that he launched his Asian campaign in 333BC, just three years after Darius had assumed the Persian throne at the age of 45. The Macedonian led the invasion of the Persian Empire, he said, to rid the world of oppression and tyranny, but in the back of his mind was the Persian invasion of Greece almost 150 years earlier. He knew that ineffective kings and many rebellions had weakened the Persian empire, as well as corruption and palace and harem intrigues. And he knew Darius was desperately trying to strengthen his army.

Darius and his Persian army took up high positions on the banks of the Granicus River, near the Aegean coast, and waited for the invaders. Alexander saw them and plunged his cavalry into the surging river and up the steep embankments. In savage, hand-to-hand combat, the Persians were defeated, but Darius escaped to fight another day.

The Macedonians and the Persians met again at Issus, after Darius had raised a second army. In the ensuing battle, the Persians greatly outnumbered the Macedonians, but Darius was not able to take advantage of his numbers because the battlefield was a narrow mountain pass and he lacked space. Once again, the Persians were defeated, and Darius escaped.

However, Alexander entered Damascus and seized Darius's war chest and his family, although Darius was later to say that his family was treated well in captivity.

Two years later, Alexander broke off his campaign in Egypt and again pursued Darius. The Macedonian conquered all the lands between the Euphrates and Tigris rivers, including Babylon, and finally found the Persian Army on the plains of Guagamela. Once again, despite savage fighting, the Persians were slaughtered. Only strategic bungling on the part of one of Alexander's generals allowed Darius to escape once again.

#

Over the centuries, when Persian kings ruled a mighty empire in Western Asia, massive riches had poured into the royal treasury from taxes and from plunder and tribute from conquered nations and cities everywhere. In addition, the Persian treasurers had developed a system of economics and of personal and community wealth that greatly added to the empire's riches. If the people can be shown how to be rich, the treasurers argued, the empire will be rich - and they were proved right.

The wealth of the empire was evident to all who approached its cities. Massive murals depicted deposed kings bearing their annual tribute to the Persian rulers on the occasion of the New Year's feast. The palaces were splendid beyond belief.

The magnificent palace complex at Persepolis sat at the foot of Kuh-i-Rahmat, or "Mountain of Mercy", in the plain of Marv Dasht, 400 miles south of the present capital of Iran, Teheran. It was built by another Darius, Darius the Great, 200 years earlier. It took a century to complete.

The Wealth of Persepolis

What the early historians wrote about the wealth of Persepolis was not exaggerated. The Greek historian Diodorus Siculus reported that Persepolis was "the wealthiest city under the sun", and her houses were full of gold and silver and all sorts of riches, including furniture and precious objects of every kind. The women had many expensive dresses, embroidered with purple or with gold, and splendid were the costumes of the priests and nobles of the empire.

However, as the empire staggered under the weight of uprisings, corruption, assassinations and palace intrigues, the treasury began to hoard its wealth and the economy began to stagnate.

And when Alexander took Persepolis, he ransacked and looted the treasury. The treasure from this city alone, according to the historian Plutarch, was so great it had to be carried away on 20,000 mules and 5000 camels. In silver alone, 2500 tons were found in Persepolis and the whole vast treasure had to be sent in great convoys north to the city of Susa to be kept under close guard.

Inexhaustible Greed

Alexander's soldiers were allowed to ransack the houses of Persepolis, where they killed the men and carried away all the booty they could carry. The Macedonians were said to have spent the whole day in pillage, but still could not satisfy their inexhaustible greed. They dragged the women away with their jewels and treated all their captives as slaves.

Alexander's vengeance did not stop there. He wanted the Persians to truly pay for their invasion of Greece 150 years earlier. He held games and offered sacrifices to the gods and entertained his officers and friends lavishly. At one such drunken orgy, it is said, an Athenian courtesan, called Thais, tempted the drunken Alexander. She said it would be his greatest achievement in Asia to lead a procession in Persepolis to the Palace of Xerxes (a former king of Persia) and set fire to it. The assembly rose in drunken cheer and lurched to the palace, and this woman, Thais, threw the second torch, after Alexander's, into the buildings. Thus it was, history records, that Athens was avenged by a single woman, destroying in an instant of madness what had been the pride of the Persians.

Persepolis had certainly exceeded all other cities in riches, but now she surpassed them all in misfortune.

\#

Alexander then pushed for hundreds of miles north along the mountains towards the Caspian Sea, where Darius and his soldiers were believed to be encamped in his summer palace. When the Macedonian arrived, however, he found the Persian king dead in his coach. Darius had been assassinated by the commander of his own Bactrian cavalry, Bessus. Moved by the sight of the fallen king, who had fought so valiantly against him, Alexander quietly covered him with his cloak.

Alexander chased Bessus and captured him. The Persian was brought naked in bonds and a wooden collar to stand before Alexander in Bactra. Alexander asked him why he had killed his king and kinsman. Bessus was unable to justify his actions and he was flogged, a Macedonian traditional punishment. Then, in keeping with Persian tradition, his nose and ears were cut off. After being tried by a Persian court, he was executed.

Alexander gave Darius, his great foe, a royal funeral.

Alexander had done a very thorough job of looting the royal storehouse of the treasury, and excavations, by the Oriental Institute of the University of Chicago and others, more than two thousand years later, found only objects overlooked or dropped accidentally by the departing Macedonians.

Many of these finds were pieces of booty from wars with nations like Greece, Egypt and India, and tribute from various subject nations.

Hundreds of clay tablets were also uncovered in the debris, with inscriptions in Elamite cuneiform. These had been originally sun-dried, but had been baked in the immense heat from the fires lit by Alexander, so that many were found intact instead of having crumbled to dust in ages past.

These tablets, written mostly in Old Persian and translations of Elamite and Babylonian, proved to be of great value to archaeologists. They tell of skilled workers from all over the empire, among them stone-relief and inscription workers from Egypt, goldsmiths from Caria and ornament makers from Susa. They show records, including details of money given to workers for their labor. They tell of sales records, land and property deals, taxes to be paid, and amounts of money borrowed from the treasury and money lenders.

Thus Alexander, by chance, left treasure of a different kind for future generations.

That, so history tells us, is the true background to the fall of Persepolis. Now let us relate the legend of one man among the many in Persepolis in those last days, a story written by the man himself and preserved, unintentionally, by Alexander the Great when he burned the Palace of Xerxes to the ground.

Among the clay tablets of Persepolis, so the story goes, were a number written by a high treasury official, one Tragoas, who acknowledged himself to be the richest man in Persia. He is believed to have hastily dictated the Persian Empire's wealth creation secrets to scribes as Alexander and his 60,000 men marched towards Persepolis.

Why would he have done so? Why would he not have scooped up his treasure and escaped? Why would he risk his life to record the secrets of financial riches when he was already a wealthy man - in fact, the richest in Persia?

We do not need to look beyond his own words to establish his motivation. These words will give us a good idea of the kind of man he was and what was going through his mind in those dying days of the empire.

Creating Real Riches

Tragoas apparently had to rush from the city as Alexander marched in, leaving his tablets behind. What must his thoughts have been as he saw his beloved city in flames?

Whatever his thoughts, he left behind as his enduring legacy perhaps the most extraordinary concepts for making money and creating real riches as have ever been devised.

And you will read that Tragoas had a higher purpose in desperately wanting to change attitudes towards money. Could it be that the Great God of the Persians had a hand in the recent discovery of these ancient tablets? Could it be that they were discovered now because they are needed now - now more than ever?

At a time when that ancient country, now called Iran, is at odds with Western powers, does it still have a message that the Western world desperately needs?

Yes, these steps to riches were written more than two thousand years ago, and devised long before that. But read them and see for yourself whether they apply just as much today as they did then. In fact, would not these principles, used in conjunction with today's techniques and technologies, be even more potent?

Read on. There can surely be no-one alive, no matter how poor in spirit or in money, who would not be enriched, and enriched enormously, by the wisdom of the Richest Man in Persia.

BRIAN MORGAN

The Testimony of Tragoas

I, Tragoas, official of the Great Treasury of the greatest city of Persia, Persepolis, greet those fortunate enough to read the Codes of Riches, as depicted on these clay tablets - and use them to accumulate great wealth. Let it be known that all are free to do so.

Many, even the Great King Darius himself, have called me the Richest Man in Persia, and none have disputed this claim. I am happy to accept the honor because I am indeed rich - and rich in more ways than one.

Would that I could tell you all, but I must not tarry. That arrogant invader, Alexander the Macedonian, is marching from Susa to Persepolis with 60,000 men - and he will be ruthless, make no mistake, after the king's valiant efforts to turn him back.

He will smash the doors of the Treasury and carry away as booty the untold riches therein, as he has done everywhere else his heavy foot has trod. Thus will Persia crumble.

But I must do what I can to show future generations how to restore lost wealth and lost morals. I must record the secrets of the ancients, so that those who follow can once again gather riches for themselves and so make the whole world richer for their efforts. For is it not so that the world is richer for every rich citizen in it? And, in a sane world, can we ever again allow greed to corrupt and destroy the world?

Wounds heal with time. Shame can be tamed by those with integrity and purpose. I have lived the good life. I have been blessed by the Great God, but I may be called to join him before this day is out. My purpose now is to shine my lamp on the efforts of the past, so that the future may be full of hope and triumph for those who come after me.

Thus, as quickly as the scribes can record these ancient Codes, I will flee this city of my youth or give my final breath for those who follow. May future generations share the great abundance from the Great God.

#

Although in recent times the rose has wilted, the Persian Empire has been the greatest the world has known, and incomparable has been its riches.

Now let it be known that I do not speak only of wealth as measured in gold. No, my friends, I speak of much more than this, for riches embrace much more than gold. *Much more*. And I speak of the quest for *real* riches.

When our ancestors conquered Assyria and Babylon and Egypt and all of the other cities and nations, they did not destroy everything they found. They searched out the best each city had in wealth, yes, but also in beauty, in art and artifacts, in laws, in the leisure arts, in agriculture, in philosophy and teachings, and in skills of all kinds, including the skills of the artisans and workers.

Unsurpassed was the bounty gathered by the ancestors, bounty matched only by the wisdom of those forefathers in knowing what to do with all those riches.

If a man hoards money, he will gradually become rich, but he will not be truly happy, and he will be on constant guard because he will be afraid of losing his wealth and he might have made many enemies as he trampled over people for his own gain.

A Culture of Greed

If a nation hoards its riches, a culture of greed will be encouraged, in which the few become rich and the many become poor. And greed will drive an ever-growing wedge between rich and poor. If only the few are striving to increase wealth, and those who are poor in money are also poor in spirit, the vast human resources of the nation are wasted and true abundance is lost.

The same can be said of an empire and the same can be said of riches of all kinds, how ever they are measured.

So the forefathers knew what must be done to increase the great bounty they gathered as the empire grew. And, as strange as it may seem to those unaccustomed to the ways of abundance, they knew that, to multiply riches, they had to give them away.

I will say that again. *To multiply riches, they had to give them away.*

And that is why the empire became great. We Persians developed a single rule of law throughout the empire, so that all were equal before it. We spread a heritage of art and beauty and learning throughout the world, so that the whole world could benefit from the gains Persians had made.

A Vast Treasure

And, though our fathers keep a vast treasure in the Treasury for the good of the empire and to protect it, they also used wealth for the good of the people and encouraged all citizens from all the cities of the world to seek riches, for the greater the number of rich people there are in the world, the greater will be the abundance and the opportunity created for all.

Money multiplies in wondrous ways according to the number of hands that hold it - wondrous ways that mystify even the magicians and sorcerers. Money breeds abundance, even as the hares in the fields multiply.

I say all this so that you will understand the abundance and opportunity that awaited me as a young man and was still there later in life as I encountered obstacles and finally lost my fortune and had to start again. Abundance will always exist for those who seek it.

In taking opportunities to seek wealth, I was able to show others the way to wealth, so that, although I partook of the abundance available to me, the abundance was not diminished because of me - it became greater.

\#

Although I became much traveled as my stature and influence as a trader and property owner and a man of wealth grew, I am proud that I have always called Persepolis home. It breaks my heart that I have had to send my family away, and I must try to follow as the Macedonian approaches our gates. But what I hasten to inscribe on these tablets is of greater importance than a single man or a single city.

The world must know what I know. Only then will I have done my duty and only then will my worth as a citizen be fulfilled.

Let it be understood that, whatever your circumstances and whatever your city, to become all that you might as a citizen, you must do whatever you can, with whatever you have, starting in your own city, right now. There is fortune to be made in your city, as there was in mine. Yes, my city is magnificent, but, wherever there are citizens who have needs, there are opportunities.

My Road to Riches

But this is *my* testimony, and I must speak of *my* road to riches, starting in *my* city.

The kings of Persia have always used Persepolis as their capital for the New Year festivities as spring bursts forth each year. They knew that spring symbolizes renewal, a fresh start, a surge of energy after the cold and gloom of winter. It symbolizes that bad times have an end and good times come again in ways that quicken the blood and lift the spirits.

King Cyrus, he who conquered Babylon, established his capital, the Camp of the Persians, near Persepolis. His tomb is still here, its white limestone glistening in the sun and the sharp Persian air.

Under Darius the Great, the King of Kings, this city became famous for its walled-in gardens, with trees, pools and canals. We call such gardens "paradise", and they truly are a wonder.

All countries and all cities have their advantages and the enterprising will always seek them out. Persia lies across ancient trade routes between East and West. It is a crossroads through which rich merchants flow to the West, carrying spices, silks, embroidery, frankincense, myrrh and gold. Merchants from the West carry those things needed in the East and, if you wish to see abundance on the march, look no farther than this road. Persia is also on the sea, and Persian seamen are famous for their long voyages to seek their fortune.

The ancients of this land firmly established the golden daric coin, named after Darius, as the world's first trusted unit of exchange. Persians were both willing and able to trade.

This is my city. What is yours? What advantages does it possess? What opportunities does it offer? What riches? What do its citizens need?

And, most important of all, *what can you do for its citizens*?

\#

My story starts in shame, but, if I am to live what I preach, I must speak the truth courageously, just as, all those years ago, I had to find the courage to rise above misery and misfortune.

My youth was wasted on games and wine and carousing and idleness. I was a disgrace to my parents, who had labored long for me and showered me with every blessing. They did not deserve what I did to them. I not only abandoned them, but I abandoned the very principles and values by which they lived.

I cannot think of it now without cringing in shame, so I will pass over those sorry years quickly. My one consolation is that my parents lived long enough for their pride in me to be restored and for them to forgive me.

A Life of Indolence

No, I cannot tarry on such memories, save to say that such a lifestyle strips away all traces of dignity and self-esteem. I saw work as drudgery because I could see no virtue in it. Why should I strive for anything when a life of indolence gave me all I wanted? I had wine to drink, sport when I was sober, friends to carouse with. And my parents were always there to throw me a lifeline.

But idleness leads to boredom, boredom leads to wicked ways, wine cannot be bought without coin, and friends drift away when you begin to use them. Even parents find they must withdraw in order, eventually, to be kind.

And so, on a bitter morning, with my head pounding in pain and the sun piercing my eyes after a night of debauchery, sick in body and sick at heart, I finally resolved to make something of my miserable life.

Even the Great God will not change the past. Only the future can compensate for it.

I shall spare you the details of the weeks and months that followed as I tried to find work and to wipe away my parents' shame. Suffice to say that my reputation preceded me everywhere I turned and no-one would give me work. Finally I realized that, *if my life was to change, it would be up to me, not somebody else.* By this tortuous path I came to the conclusion that I must find my own ways of earning coins.

What Could I Do?

But what could I do? I had no skills. I had nothing but the robes on my back and the worn sandals on my feet. If my parents had not fed me, I might have starved.

I had to cast off my rags. I had to find a better life.

So I began to look for something I could do to earn coins that required no money to start, no skills, no tools or equipment. I could not buy goods to sell to others, so I thought I would have to either obtain goods without cost or simply offer a service of some kind. Either way, the free goods or the service would have to have sufficient value for someone else to part with hard-earned coin to obtain them.

When I had almost given up hope, the answer came to me in a crowded market place on the shrill cry of a vendor.

"Water!" he cried. "Slacken your thirst with cool water. The elixir of life. Water for parched throats and only one copper from your purse!"

My heart pounded. Water. What else was more scarce or more precious in this harsh land of dust and heat? Could I not sell water? I could sew a goatskin to hold it. I was willing to work, to carry the water from the stream to the market. I would not grow rich this way, but it would be a start.

And so I started, and I did not grow rich.

I Did Not Grow Rich

I toiled to carry the water to the market and then stood all day in the sun and wind and dust, crying to passers-by until my own throat croaked and I drank away my livelihood. I did make some coins, the first in my life earned in honest toil, and this made me feel better about myself. But it was hard work, long hours, for little return.

I was tempted, so very tempted, to give up. But my father saw my struggle and spoke to me at the end of a particularly discouraging day.

"I can see how down-hearted you are, Tragoas," he said, offering me a tray of citrus fruit and nuts. I had not the strength nor the will to reply. He sat for a while and spoke again.

"It seems to me that the Great God sent you water as an opportunity when you were at your lowest ebb," he said. "You can do one of two things with it. You can walk away and look for something else, or you can look for ways to make it work."

"Make it work?" What could he be talking about? Had I not worked myself to a standstill?

You Must Do Three Things

"Well," he said, "for your idea of water supply to work, you must do three things. You must make your service of such value that more people will pay for it, and you must make sure that the profit you make out of it is worth the effort you put into it."

I snapped. "Even a sheep would understand such things."

I saw the hurt in my father's eyes and felt again the shame of earlier days.

"Forgive me, father," I said. "You are right. I should think more on these things. But you said there were three things necessary to make my idea work. I must increase the value and make the profits adequate. But what is the third thing?"

My father smiled and said nothing for what seemed a long time. Then he put his hand on my shoulder and looked into my eyes, as he did when he wanted to make sure he had my attention.

"Tragoas," he said, at last, "sometimes the best way to make money is to *help others make money*."

#

As sometimes happens when you think of a problem long enough, the answer came to me suddenly two days later as I sat in the sun plying my trade. When I rushed home to tell my father of my plan to help others make money, I found him in the company of an old friend, Ramazan, a Master Weaver, a man well accustomed to the life of a trader.

Both men were delighted with my simple plan, and both offered to help. From my father came the gift of an old, black, goat-hair tent and some shade cloth. From his friend, Ramazan, a week later, came a woven banner, boldly proclaiming the words: "Tragoas the Trader".

I was more than a little embarrassed at the banner, but he urged me to take it and use it, because, as he said, a trader is only as good as his name and his reputation.

"With your name on high for all to see," he said, "you will be encouraged to strive for a reputation of honesty and integrity. If your name is trusted, your reputation will spread from mouth to mouth and people will be willing to buy from you. A good name leads to prosperity for you and satisfaction for all who buy from you."

So, I set up my tent in a busy part of the city and flew my banner on high. Here I was able to offer my customers shade in which to quench their thirst and a cooler drink because the sun no longer warmed the goatskins.

Soon I was able to employ an old friend to carry the water for me on his donkey. But it was no longer water from the stream. I remembered, from my carefree, wandering days, a clear spring that bubbled from rocks high in the hills and this is the water my carter brought to my tent.

Offer Greater Value

At the same time, I employed four youths, plus a one-armed man, who had been unable to find work, and a destitute widow to sell the water from six locations in the city, each sheltered under shade cloth. Thus, I could offer greater value through cooler, fresher water (spring, not stream), shade and convenient locations. Soon all six locations carried the "Tragoas the Trader" banner and my reputation grew.

Rich people were now buying whole goatskins of my water, such was its quality, and I employed another man to carry water from the hills. I found that, by finding water of greater value, I had effectively by-passed the competition among water vendors and set myself apart.

By chance, I had discovered an important principle: *value overcomes competition*.

I did not receive more money from a goatskin of water, but I sold many more of them, so there was plenty of money for the carters and the vendors. There was even enough by then to employ a steward to run my trading business for me.

I was now earning money without actually working in the business myself. My parents were very proud of the turn-around in my life. And so was I.

When my father saw that I was both mentally and physically determined to succeed, and to succeed by helping others to succeed, he and his friend, Ramazan, began to teach me the skills and insights they themselves had learned from studying the ways of the ancients.

The Ethical Way to Riches

Everything that follows of the ethical way to riches I owe to them, and to the wise men who trod the path before them.

In recent times, corruption and palace intrigues have sullied the proud names of Persia and led to greed and hoarding of wealth. Now I fear that, in the scramble for wealth after the Macedonian breaches our gates, plunders our city and leaves it in ruins, the higher purposes of life will be entirely forgotten. If they are, then perhaps one day these hurried words of mine might turn people back towards enlightenment.

#

"The stream of water from your spring has set you free from the bondage of poverty," my father said one day. "Now you must turn your thoughts to other things, else your hard-earned money will flow away as quickly and easily as your water flows."

"But surely I must watch my business diligently to see that this does not happen." I was a little confused by my father's words.

"Your trading has been successful because your high-value service was fresh and new," he said. "But a business must always remain fresh and new. A tree grows from moist roots, but rotting wood produces nothing."

Now I was more confused than ever.

"Your water service will prosper as long as people want it, and as long as they need to buy from you. But what if the spring dries up? What if others find your spring, or other springs, and set up in opposition? Many unforeseen things can happen to pull the rug out from under unprepared feet. Always look for ideas that will keep your service fresh."

Ramazan was smiling as he watched me from under his bushy eyebrows.

"Your father is right," he said. "You must not allow yourself to fall into a position where your livelihood, and that of your workers, relies on just one thing. *To be truly successful, you must always seek additional streams of income to increase the flow of your river of riches."*

Suddenly I understood.

"You still have little money to put into your business," Ramazan said. "However, there is another way, a time-honored way, to make money. You now have six stands in the city, plus your tent, selling your water. Why not make better use of them?" He paused again. "Why not use them to *bring buyer and seller together?*"

At first, I didn't realize what he had said, but then the beautiful simplicity of the plan struck me. There were always people wanting to sell things, and people willing to buy, but they could not always find each other easily. If I could bring them together, if I could thereby find other goods for my water vendors to trade, the vendors would earn more, the suppliers would sell more, the buyers would find what they wanted and everyone would be happy. I let out a yell of joy.

When I settled down, Ramazan spoke.

"I spend my days teaching my students to be skilled weavers," Ramazan said. "All day they sit at ancient looms, weaving the red, green and yellow silks into vibrant bedcovers and other cloths. They also make *yazdi*, a heavy silk cloth decorated with birds and intricate designs. The women of the city love these things, but I need more ways for the women to find them. You have proved yourself to be an honest man, Tragoas. I am more than willing for you to take what my weavers produce to offer them in the market."

And so, expansion began

And so, expansion of my business began, with woven cloths and silks on display under my enlarged shade cloth shelters and two people now employed at each stand to look after the needs of more buyers. My manager was now busy with double the number of workers, larger display sites and increasing trade.

To make my testimony complete, I should say that the young widow who became one of my first water vendors proved to be hard-working, honest and full of ideas that enhanced the business. We worked together to solve many problems and to create opportunities. Through her, we began to find work for other women in desperate circumstances, who also proved worthy of the trust we placed in them. Yes, Minab, who was named thus because she was born near the sea, became my confidant and, eventually, my beloved. How can I describe to you the joy the Great God showered upon me on that day I realized my love for her was returned. Suffice to say that we were soon married with my parents' blessing. Minab is now the mother of my children and grandmother to my grandchildren and I cannot do without her. I will hasten to join her when this testimony is complete. However, future generations should know that a life dedicated to higher purposes and ideals attracts undreamed of blessings. My beautiful Minab is a blessing unequaled in my lifetime. May such joy be yours.

But I must return to my story. Time is short.

We were still using donkeys at that time to cart water and I began to use horses and camels to bring woven cloths to market. As the years passed, my knowledge of these animals increased and I also began to trade in animals, adding another stream to my river of riches.

By this time, we were selling goatskins of spring water to those who desired it, but we freely gave cool drinks to those who stopped at our stalls to look at our goods. Indeed, we began to offer free drinks to all who were thirsty because it made us feel good to do so. To our surprise, this attracted more people to look at our goods, so, by giving freely, we received, and we took this lesson to heart in all aspects of our business

To receive, we decided, *we must be prepared to give*.

One day, a traveler stopped at my tent (by now much larger, with curtained partitions to separate different goods). This simple courtesy of a free drink, offered in friendship, was much appreciated and the traveler was so grateful he gave me information that added another surging stream to my river of riches. He told me there was much salt in the mountains along the Silk Road to the north-west. All that was needed, he said, was the means of carting it to those who needed it.

It proved, of course, to be a little more complex than that, but soon treaties were forged with leaders of that far-off land and men began to cut blocks of salt, ready for my donkeys. There was more salt than I could handle, and soon my many donkey teams were passing each other on the Silk Road as they brought back much-needed salt to villages near and far.

I should say that the traveler who set me on the road to salt riches had not asked me for anything in return. His information was in return for my simple generosity. Now I had an opportunity to repay his generosity, and I did so by rewarding him with part of all the gold I earned from that salt. The Great God had provided the abundance of salt, and I honored that abundance by spreading it to as many people as possible. It gave Minab and me very great satisfaction to live our lives in this way.

The Generosity Story

I thought this would be the end of the generosity story, but it was not so. Word spread of the various generous deeds offered under the banner of Tragoas the Trader, and more people were attracted to buy from us, which meant we had more to share and the cycle of abundance and generosity continued. And all the time, Minab and I were growing richer, no matter how much we shared.

"You have done very well," my father said one day. "You have filled the needs of many people with goods and services of exceptional value. You have given honest work to many people and encouraged them to develop their skills to earn more money. And you have honored the Great God with your generosity."

My father's praise was such a far cry from his disappointment of many years ago.

"I wonder if you realize what you have done with your donkey teams and other aspects of your business?" he said.

I thought that I had simply seized opportunities when I saw them, found people and animals to make them work, and filled basic human needs for salt and other goods. But I could tell from the twinkle in my father's eye that I had somehow managed to do more than that.

"You found, for example, that a donkey team and a cart could make money hauling salt to the villages," he said. "You then found that two teams could double your business, four could double it again, eight could double it again, and on and on. This meant several things. It meant you had back-up if men were hurt or ill, and also your increasing strengths discouraged others from competing with you. However, what is more important, you discovered the most basic rule of business, but the one that is most overlooked."

My father stopped and sipped his citrus juice. I knew he was waiting for me to absorb what he had said. When I still looked confused, he explained.

The Basic Rule of Business

"When you work for yourself, the greater your success, the harder you work. This is because you *are* the business and it cannot operate without you. You cannot take a holiday or become sick; too much depends on you being there."

He paused and put his hand on my shoulder, making sure I understood what he was saying.

"A business must be set up so that it can be replicated. All parts of the business must be capable of being undertaken by someone else. If a business is capable of replication, and proves itself to be profitable in this arrangement, there is little to stand between you and your fortune."

A business must be capable of replication.

It was as if he had lit a lamp in a dark room. By chance, by attempting merely to help others make a living, I had been making my various businesses, and each part of them, replicable. They were operating whether I was present or not, but I had not been taking full advantage of it.

I realized now that, if I knew how to create businesses in my city and how to create work for people, and I knew what worked and what did not, then surely I could set up the same businesses in other cities and towns and help more people. If I knew how to replicate, why not replicate? Surely this was the safe, sure way to multiply success?

My father called this one way of using *leverage*. When I look blank, he spoke of the Egyptians building the pyramids and the Babylonians lifting water from the river to their famous hanging gardens.

"Using a lever," he said, "something to lift with, a small man can move a great boulder, or raise water from its natural level. Or a man, using a different type of lever, can create great wealth."

Excitement and Expectation

From that day, I rose every morning with feelings of excitement and expectation surging through me, like a river through a narrow pass. And so, with the help of men and women experienced in my businesses, I started a program of expansion to other cities. The money lenders were keen to become part of the expansion of a business that had already proved successful, and they were very happy to lend to me, because I had proved myself reliable and honest.

My first expansion was to Susa (now effectively shut down by the Macedonian), but, within a few years, the banner of Tragoas the Trader was flying in many cities and towns, fulfilling needs and giving work to the willing.

My parents were by now quite old and I was very pleased that, because I had turned my life around, I was able to offer them much peace and every comfort in their old age. And Minab and I were delighted to present them with children and grandchildren for their pleasure and enjoyment.

My life was complete.

Complete, that is, until the day a messenger rushed to my door, sweating and out of breath. My animals had gone from their yards and my merchandise had gone from my tent. My manager and two of my workers, all trusted men, had gone, and with them, presumably, much of my money.

Betrayal and loss hit me like a fall from a runaway horse.

#

Despite initial shock, disaster sometimes rumbles in like a slow-moving elephant and you don't realize its full impact until it has trampled through your life.

Realization of separate tragedies hit me one by one. I realized that I owed money, a great deal of money. The lever of debt can do wondrous things, but there is always risk.

I had purchased a dwelling for my family using money borrowed from the money lenders. How could I repay them? I had borrowed heavily for the expansion of the business into other cities and towns and for goods now lost. How could I repay that? And, most important of all, I was ashamed to realize that I would not be able to pay the people who worked for me and relied upon me for the food their families ate and the clothes on their backs.

I sank into a misery even deeper than that of my youth. It was deeper because I had no strength, no will to find a way out of my difficulties. I could not think. I could not face my people. I forced myself out of bed each morning only because I needed to get away and I spent much time by the river alone, absorbed in the tragedy that had befallen me and in my own misery. Despair is a deep, dark hole, with no way out. Unless you have experienced such agony, or until you do, I do not expect you to fully understand.

I Felt Powerless

I tried to respond to the family around me, but I had let them down and I felt powerless to do anything about it. In my despondency, I could not add two and two together. I could not make decisions. Such effort left me confused and deep in despair. I did not know what to do.

One morning as I sat by the river feeling very alone, I was startled by a voice behind me.

"A man does not drown by falling in the river, Tragoas," my father's voice said. "He drowns by staying there."

I looked around and there was a group of people, seven in all, standing behind me. There was my father, my wife Minab, and five of the people who had worked for me.

"You have given a great deal to many people, Tragoas," my father said. "We have been talking. We have some ideas for you. We want to help you rebuild. We have appointed ourselves as your Circle of Counselors for as long as you want us or until such time as you find others more worthy."

I greeted them all as best I could, but my heart was not in it. My wife saw my discomfort and spoke.

"My dear husband," she said, "you took me from abject poverty and gave me work. You trusted me and gave me positions of responsibility. You gave me your love and married me. You gave me our children. You have given every comfort and blessing to your parents in their old age. All of the people here and many others have had work because of you and have been able to feed and clothe their families and provide a roof over their heads. Many, many people are better off because of you. It's time we helped you return to what you were."

The Three-step Plan

I embraced my wife then, in front of those present, and I am not ashamed to say that I wept openly before them. My father, after a time, spoke again.

"Tragoas, all progress evolves from discontent or disaster, and determination to overcome them. We have developed a three-step plan to try to restart your business. The steps are very simple, but each are essential if you are to succeed. Are you willing to listen?"

I nodded, but I still could not speak.

"The first step is to send out emissaries without delay to all the cities, towns and villages where you have conducted business," he said. "We have assumed that all is lost. It may not be so. If we send emissaries wherever you have traded, then perhaps there are parts of your business that are still operating or that can be started again."

I sat up. He was right. How stupid I had been.

"The second step," he said, "is to create a plan for restarting the business using the knowledge handed down by the ancients and the knowledge you have gathered yourself over the years in establishing your business."

The others were smiling now.

"The third step is to call two gatherings. One will be for your workers in each city to tell them of your plans to restart and seek their help. You might be surprised by their eagerness to work again. The second gathering would be for others who are part of your business. These would include the people who supply you with goods, especially those to whom you owe money, and also the money lenders. At this gathering, you can tell them of your plan to rebuild."

It all made sense, even to my befuddled mind. There may well, indeed, be parts of the business still working, or some that could be started again with little effort. Clearly, to go forward we could only succeed with a fresh, new plan, and we needed all of the people who had an interest in the business to become part of that plan and, most important of all, to approve it.

My Circle of Counselors

Perhaps there was a way out, after all. My father always said that, when it becomes dark enough, you can see the stars. I splashed some water in my face, but my mind was already beginning to clear. At last, I spoke to them.

"I am by no means convinced that I deserve your trust and friendship, but I can tell you," I paused as my voice began to betray me, "I can tell you, I most deeply appreciate it. We shall do as you say. We shall implement the three-step plan. But first

I will take the intermediate step. I will first most gratefully accept you as my Circle of Counselors and wonder why I never did so before. Clearly, many minds are better than one and *no-one can be truly successful alone*. I certainly cannot. My father and his friend, Ramazan, have been my masters in the art of business, and I have learnt from them as they learnt from the forefathers. Now each of us must put our best efforts into rebuilding this business and, in so doing, creating other masters who can pass on these skills to future generations. The more people we help, the more our business will grow. If I am convinced of anything, I am convinced of that."

And so, emissaries were sent in all directions, to every city and town where we had done business, to seek out those who had worked for us, to warn them about the men who had betrayed us and to appoint leaders to care for the business, at least until a new manager was appointed. In each city, they were also told of the plans to rebuild, and, almost without exception, they chose to stay with us.

Emissaries were also sent to the suppliers and money lenders to invite them to a gathering at the Tragoas tent, which still stood in the Persepolis market, to discuss our plan for a fresh start. In the meantime, the counselors and I sat down every day to talk about what we wanted to do and how we should do it, gradually developing a plan of action.

As each emissary returned with news, we were able to adjust our plan accordingly. We found, for example, that most of the donkey teams were still operating to the north, carting salt to villages. They had been spread so far, many did not know of the tragedy that had struck us. We found that everything at Susa had gone. We were too slow. Those who betrayed us at Persepolis also betrayed us at Susa and other places, simply because I had allowed myself to become mired in self-pity. I had allowed it to happen. But many of the towns and villages were still operating much as before. Wherever business could operate, new people were appointed to take charge and make decisions so that some people could be kept in work and some money generated.

The Value of Strategy

"Now you see the value of having many streams of income in your river of riches." My father looked at Ramazan and smiled as he remembered the time they had first suggested this strategy to me many years ago.

Looking back now, I realized that my trading business had grown without sufficient thought, responding to problems or opportunities as they arose. I realized how much more successful we could be if we started afresh with proper forethought and a simple plan based on established knowledge and skills.

When we finally met the money lenders and suppliers at Persepolis, we were able to present to them a full plan that they accepted readily. The money lenders wanted previous loans paid back and they also wanted to lend more. After all, that was the reason they were in business. They recognized our business methods had been successful and our new plan would prove more successful still. The suppliers wanted to keep supplying us and they wanted payment for previous supplies, and they realized that the only way to achieve that was for us to stay in business. They, also, readily accepted the plan.

The trust we had built up over many years now saved us from disaster.

The people who had worked for me were glad of the opportunity to work again. All agreed, if we all worked hard, in accordance with the new plan, everyone would benefit.

Indeed, the very theme of our plan attracted everybody to it: *"Creating abundance in order to give and to serve."*

#

From the depths of my winter, I had finally found a spring of endless possibility. And in such a frame of mind, it was probably inevitable that I was able to quickly restart my life as a trader. Rebuilding, indeed, proved to be much easier than becoming established when I was young.

Back then, it was a matter of trial and error, as I moved from one idea to another to find what would work. Now it was different, but the credit for my ability to start again, and start again so quickly, should be given to three things.

The first was that I was able to firmly establish in my mind *the ardent desire* to not only start again, but to surpass anything I had done before. It is true that, to master wealth, *first you must master your mind*.

The Power of People

The second was my realization that, to succeed, I had to accept, indeed invite, the help of other people. Once I realized that, I wondered how I had ever succeeded before. Then I remembered that I had, in fact, accepted help. Had not my father and Ramazan become my masters, willing to teach me the proven ways of old? Had I not consulted with and worked with Minab? Had I not been helped by many workers? Had not the money lenders and suppliers supported my efforts?

All this was true, of course, but now I realized I could do better. Now my masters had been joined by Minab and five others to become my Circle of Counselors. Their advice and guidance would surely be invaluable and a resource to treasure. In addition, if I sought advice and ideas from all my suppliers and workers and even buyers, and rewarded them for any useful ideas, would I not be sitting on a treasure trove that would become many streams of income flowing into my river of riches? In addition, thanks to Minab, I now realized that I had not done enough to encourage women to become part of my business. Were not women stronger than they look, loyal, clever and honest? Do not women hold up half of the sky?

Honesty and Integrity

The third thing that helped me establish again quickly was my determination to honor the trust placed in me by the money lenders by *always acting with honesty and integrity*. I would do this by filling needs, by creating abundance and by sharing with open-hearted generosity.

Where others acted with deception, I would act with honesty. Where others acted without a care for people, I would put people first. Where others acted with greed, I would give. I would give from all of my resources. I would give of my treasure. I would give of myself. And I would encourage and reward any of my workers who chose to adopt the same philosophy.

I would be cautious, of course. I had been bitten once. But I would not set my own standards in business or elsewhere in accordance with the standards of other people. My purpose in life was a matter between me and the Great God.

Let others scoff. I would surely stand tall in the sight of the Great God, if no-one else. I would sleep well at night with a clear conscience. And I would one day go to my eternal rest without regret.

This I believed - and, in this belief, so I acted.

#

Life became very busy and very soon my business was restored to what it was, and money began to flow back to the money lenders. I set up a system of controls, so that it would be very difficult for anyone to steal from me again. I vowed that no-one would suffer again because of my lack of diligence.

By now, I had extended my hospitality to buyers and travelers by offering sweetmeats, fruit and cakes hot from the oven, as well as my refreshing spring water. Once again, the courtesy was returned a hundredfold.

A traveler told me of a treasure to be found far to the north, near the Caspian Sea. I hired him to take me there, and found an amazing sight - a fountain spouting oil into the air in great quantities.

"This oil is good to burn," my new friend said, "and is also used to anoint camels for the itch."

Finding New Uses

Indeed it was, but, in time, I found many more uses for it. Is this not an easy way to find additional income streams - simply by *finding new uses for existing goods*?

The people of China, for example, prized the oil as a great balm for body and soul, and took as much as I could carry to them. Thus did my donkey teams earn double for me, and for the workers. Traveling east, they carried oil. Traveling west, they carried salt.

In keeping with my plan, I rewarded the traveler who found the oil, and the people of the Caspian Sea, out of my profits. These profits were so great that, within a few years, I purchased several large reed huts and built a safe compound, where I employed women to care for homeless children, orphaned by war and other tragedies. There were many such children in those parts, and great was our joy in caring for them. The women I chose to care for the children were themselves widows. They understood suffering, they knew the ways of nurturing children, and so they were ideal for the work and were thus able to provide for their own families. I encouraged the women to pass on to the children our philosophy of giving, hoping that, one day, they might work with us in the business. In this way, our care could stretch for a lifetime.

Every year, I increased the merchandise on display under my banners. There were drinking cups for the wealthy, finished in gold. There was pottery in all shapes and sizes, some with birds, animals or intricate patterns painted black on a red background - beautiful to behold.

Properties Grew in Value

No longer could I fit my merchandise under simple shade cloth. I still had some tents, but now I was purchasing buildings within various cities and towns to better display goods and make them secure from thieves. Thus was my wealth growing by another stream as these properties grew in value.

I was concentrating on purchasing things that increased in value and making sure that what I borrowed was used for this purpose and not for things that decreased in value.

Now I had suitable places to display colorful carpets and rugs, spread on brick floors, their patterns of lustrous flowers and plant tendrils attracting the buyers. My caravans carried fine carpets from the northern bazaars to sell alongside our Persian stock, and cloths of silk in crimson and other beautiful and rich colors to display beside Ramazan's fine wares.

Women in the marketplace told us they wanted the pleasure of jewelry, so we tried to fill that need. From India and Ceylon I brought precious stones. I took them to the stone-polishers to improve their value so that I could sell them in my own markets and take them to far lands.

It was becoming a very complex task to keep track of my caravans, to find goods for them to carry back and forth, and to find the men and animals to operate them.

Soon my markets were full of delights and temptations for people in many cities. And everywhere I had a market, I performed some service for the people there, in the way I had established care for children near the Caspian Sea. My money helped build temples and pay teachers for children, and feed and clothe the poor. If a city had a need, I tried to fill it. All this was done without thought of reward, but rewarded I was, when people flocked to my markets because they knew my name.

There they found merchandise from the far corners of the world. There were precious stones, pearls, elephant tusks, cloths of silk and gold, ruby-like spinels of great beauty. And lapis lazuli - the finest azure in the world, deep blue flecked with gold.

Unique Value

I tried always to offer merchandise and service that was *unique and that offered great value*. This became my promise to those who bought from me, and I resolved to never make such a promise unless I was certain I could keep it. If I was not certain, I would promise less and try to surprise by giving more than I promised.

From China came gold, silks, silver and copper. Copper was much sought-after as ballast in ships, so great quantities passed through my hands. I was still using the simple method of bringing buyer and seller together, particularly when opportunities came my way but I could not afford to buy the merchandise myself.

All of my caravans were now of considerable size, with many armed guards to ward off thieves. Even so, goods were carefully sent by different caravans to different markets to spread the risk. Too many people relied on me now and we were helping the citizens of too many cities to throw everything away by carelessness.

As you can imagine, the abacus boards were very busy in my warehouses, and many men and women toiled at the tally sticks to ensure that money lenders, suppliers and workers were all paid their due, and that all who should be rewarded were not forgotten.

Whatever profits could be spared, together with money from the lenders, was used to purchase more and more property. Some was used for our own purposes, some was rented out to honest people to ply their own trade, or to live in. We encouraged our own workers to buy their own home with an incentive in coins and recommendations to money lenders. Thus my workers were encouraged to increase their own wealth, and, in so doing, increase the abundance available to all.

Some of the properties we purchased were small workshops, where, before long, forges blazed and walls echoed with the clash of metal on metal. Here workers produced knives, cleavers, tongs, swords, armor, and all manner of implements, which soon found their way to markets, my own and others. The streams of income continued to increase.

I should say that water started my road to riches and one of my workers found another kind of water that soon provided another income stream, for him and me. In southern Persia, there flows a hot spring, in which people wash clothes and soak themselves. The waters flow green and shimmering between hills along a stony course under a deep blue sky. It is a place of reprieve from the high desert places full of thorn bush, although there is the smell of rotten eggs there. But the water has proved itself good for many diseases and for curing the itch, and so I had found another offering for my markets. I would never have found it, if I had not encouraged my workers to come up with ideas and to seek out opportunities.

Finding Ready Demand

From this, we found there was a ready demand for anything that would help ward off disease and illness, so I sent messengers to seek out herbs and spices that might be in demand for cooking or for medicinal purposes.

In China, they found many spices, including pepper, nutmeg, cloves and ginger, plus medicinal herbs, perfumes and dyes.

In India also, they found medicinal herbs. They found strips of cinnamon bark to chew, which was much sought-after for ailments of the heart and lungs. There were also herbs said to be good for treating potency, leprosy and snakebite, and to prevent baldness. From India came a rare plant, called indigo, whose leaves provide a rich, blue dye much praised by traders and weavers.

Down by the waters of the Persian Gulf, I found fishermen who were struggling to make a living from fishing the seas. Each dawn would find them rocking at sea in fishing boats held together by wooden pegs and coconut fiber. I employed a fishing master and began to purchase boats or have them made. The fishermen preferred to work for me because it took the uncertainty out of their lives, and my fishing master found ways to make a fleet profitable, where individual boats floundered.

More income streams. More replicable business ideas and systems.

As profits came in, I purchased more horses, donkeys and camels for cartage and trade. I expanded my markets and warehouses. I bought looms and employed people. I opened mines and employed more. And I kept buying property.

But, most of all, I kept finding ways to increase abundance by employing people, by creating wealth for myself and others, by sharing my profits, by filling needs wherever I found them.

Would that I could tell you more of how I became the richest man in Persia. How can I fit a lifetime onto a few clay tablets? If I had the time, I could not do it. But perhaps that is not a bad thing. You will find your own way, create your own experience, make your own life - and that is how it should be. I tell you my story only to show the way I tried to follow the ways of the ancients, which I will set out in the Codes that follow.

Not Rich in Money Alone

Yes, I became the richest man in Persia, but not rich in money alone. My story, written in haste, is not the full story. I became truly rich because *I always put my family first*. Those who say you cannot do this are either lying or speaking out of ignorance. I always took time to relax and to enjoy life. When I worked, I worked hard, but I made spaces in that work for things that were important to me and my family. I became rich by *living a life of integrity and honor*, so that never again would the name Tragoas be a name of shame. And, of course, I became truly rich, rich in heart, rich in soul, through giving, through creating abundance for others, through helping those in need. Wherever I found desperation, I tried to find inspiration. May the Great God be praised that I was sometimes able to do so.

And that is how I came to be asked by King Darius himself to become a high official in his Treasury. I had demonstrated that I could not only make and retain wealth, but that I could do so with honesty as my byword and by creating wealth for others at the same time. As the king himself said, I was a man to be trusted.

I say such things, not to boast, but in the hope that such values will return to the world. Alexander, by his own greed and that of his men, is making this a world of greed. This is a tragedy that will destroy countless lives and fill others with despair. If I did not keep hope in my heart, I could not write these tablets. Let hope one day return and banish greed.

There is much more to life than material possessions. I am proud to say that, after my one downfall, I never lost sight of the many blessings in my life, especially my family, and never failed to give thanks for those blessings.

But now, a messenger has reached my door. The Macedonian is on the march from Susa. I must hasten to inscribe these tablets with the Codes of Riches, which set out the proven ways of the ancients, and the ways I used for my own success in life.

I thank the Great God that I have been given time, however short, to produce these Codes. If they are found, and used, by others, my life will be made complete.

Code 1:
The Quest for Real Riches

All Persians know that wealth comes with privileges, but many do not understand that wealth also comes with responsibilities. These are two-fold:

1. *Hurt no-one in the gathering of wealth.*
2. *Gather for others as you gather for yourself.*

Those who wish to become rich must do so without harming or impoverishing other people. Far from creating scarcity for others, they must create abundance, and this abundance must be created in honest ways. The truly rich enjoy creating wealth that also enriches the lives of others. It has been truly said that the noblest motive is the public good.

Much is required of he to whom much is given.

Long ago, a Chinese sage said that, if you give a man a fish, you feed him for a day; but if you teach a man to fish, you feed him for a lifetime. A teacher affects eternity; he can never tell where his influence will stop. Share your knowledge and your good name will spread. As your good name spreads, so will your opportunities for wealth.

A big heart is a great gift to the world.

Abundance comes from helping other people enrich their lives, and so, your first reason for gathering riches must be to *have more to give*. Let it be understood that no-one was ever honored by the king for what he received. Honor has always been the reward for what has been given.

If you have it in your heart to make life better for others, and, if you follow the Codes that are necessary to create wealth, then you will have riches beyond your dreams.

If you are truly rich, and those whose paths you cross are also rich because of your actions, the world will be a richer place, and the abundance that already exists will multiply. Rich people create value for others and, in so doing, earn a reward for themselves. Rich people create work and give people better lives.

So, although it may seem strange to those not yet acquainted with the ways of the rich, to become rich, first you must give. Are not those who receive the most love, the most loving? Are not those with the most friends, the ones who offer friendship? Give what you can and much will be returned to you.

To receive a breath, first you must give one.

You have time to give, do you not? Do you not have advice, wisdom, a friendly smile to give? Give these things and they will flow back to you in abundance. Do this and you will add value to everything you do and value will return to you.

Let it be clearly understood: *no-one can become rich without also enriching others*. This has been the first lesson of wealth since before our grandfathers' grandfathers were born. Remember to plant money trees from which others may pick the fruit. Do not bake a small loaf to feed only yourself, bake a large loaf that will feed many. Only by sharing can you gain true prosperity.

To be a rich person, you must truly be a student of what makes people behave the way they do. Abundance will be yours *if you can help enough other people get what they want.* Everybody wants something. You must find out what it is and give it to them.

Money is like the opium that old men smoke in their pipes. If you observe closely, you will see that people are happy when they have money and miserable when they do not. Money is like a drug for them. Be mindful therefore of what money can do. It can be a curse, but it can also be a great force in the world and do much good, if your attitude to it is worthy. Possession of gold has ruined fewer people than the lack of it.

Money is simply a tool for getting things done. The more you have, the more you can get done. As the ancients have always said: *Money is a means to an end, not an end in itself.*

When there are less rich people to spend their money, or they are too greedy to share it, laborers are without work; merchants have few customers; people do not have enough money to buy their food and clothing; those on farms are unable to sell what they grow. Everything stagnates.

The ancients well knew that gold brings to those who possess it a change in their lives and a new responsibility. It can bring fear that you might lose it. It can bring a sense of power. It can give the ability to do good.

Understand that if you are to earn the respect of others and live in good conscience yourself, you must pay your debts regularly and on time and not purchase those things for which you are unable to pay. You must care for your family. You must prepare a Tablet of Intentions, so that the law-makers will know how you wish your family to be cared for when the Great God calls you. You must have compassion for others and help those who need it. Thus will others respect you and you will respect yourself. And thus you will not just become rich, but also much loved.

Be sure that you are the master of your gold. Gold can easily master he who possesses it, and tragedy and destitution follows.

Think about what you want. Must you have what you want every day - better robes, better food, jewelry? These things are soon gone and forgotten. Is it not better to seek assets that earn income? Gold, land, herds, merchandise, a business of your own?

Wealth is not measured by the coins a person holds; it is the income that flows in many streams into his possession. This is what you should seek, income that continues to flow whether you work or travel.

They are indeed rich whose income is superior to their expenses and whose expenses are no more than their desires. See to it that you do not desire more than you need for comfort and enjoyment of life. *Riches must not come at the cost of happiness.*

Those who amass wealth - with big houses and palaces, luxurious chariots, large herds and much travel - are not always satisfied, not always happy. In chasing riches, they often neglect their true personal desires. They neglect the things that they really want from life. They forget that which is truly important to them.

The learned astronomers say there are more stars in the universe than all the grains of sand in all the deserts of Persia. Perhaps those stars are there to remind us that *what counts most in life are the things that cannot be counted.*

Before you set your heart on money wealth, be sure that is truly what you want. Look closely at those who already possess wealth and see how happy they are. Then decide. It is not easy to find happiness within ourselves, but it can be found nowhere else. If you are rich in money, but poor in spirit, then you are poor indeed. Happiness is beyond price.

The quest for riches should never be at the expense of family or friendships, or physical and mental well-being. Money should always be used to enhance the values that are important to you. Money should never come at the cost of virtue. Nothing can be an advantage to you that makes you break your word or lose your self-respect. A good name is better than a girdle of gold, but there is no reason why you should not have both - a good name *and* a girdle of gold.

Is it not wise to plan for income streams for the years ahead, when you are no longer able to work or no longer with your family to support them? Should you not plan investments that will safely endure the years to come, yet be readily turned to coin when the time comes that they are needed? Would it not be wise to invest in a house because it is useful now and will grow in value in the future? Its sale, if necessary, will provide well for you or your family.

Your needs and dreams will change as the years pass. This is life, and even the Magi priests cannot foretell the future. Be prepared to change your goals in accordance with the changes in your dreams.

And be aware of health. The physicians will readily tell you that illness and misery are reduced as soon as your plan for riches, as determined by your goals and desires, is defined. Stress kills as surely as a sword. If lack of wealth causes stress, you owe it to your family to do something about it. But do not leap from one stress to another. *Having money work hard for you is much more important than you working hard for money.*

True satisfaction may not consist so much in getting what you want as in wanting what you get. There are many kinds of riches other than gold and silver. And many sages would argue that many are better than gold and silver. You must ponder these things and decide for yourself.

A king once offered a bag of gold to anyone who could name four things that money could not buy. One of his subjects whispered in his ear, and the king immediately ordered his stewards to bring a bag of gold. The four things that money could not buy? A baby's smile, youth after it is gone, the love of a good man or a good woman, entrance into heaven.

You will know many other things more important than money. Think of family, friends, contentment, enjoyment, serenity, a long and happy life, being at peace with the Great God. Wherever you are, there is beauty beyond price.

How much money would it take for you to give up your eyes, or even one of them? What is an arm worth, or a leg? How much money would you take to give up a child, any child? On your deathbed, as you are about to take your last breath, how much would you give for just one more day of health? No, my friends, there are many, many things more important than money.

The sage Socrates once declared that the human race gives most attention to the least important things and the least attention to the most important things. Wealth does not bring about excellence, he said, but excellence brings about wealth and all other public and private blessings. The most important thing was the inner state of a person's soul, Socrates said. When we attain inner excellence, outer excellence will follow - and with it, all manner of riches.

Do not sell your soul to buy your mansion.

Riches obtain their value from the attitude of those who possess them. Riches are blessings for those who know how to make them and use them, curses for those who do not.

The real good is that which you feel, not that which you can display.

The happiest people are those who derive rewards from what they contribute to life, what they contribute to others. Money is a currency for trading value or benefits. You will start to attract more money when you begin to think, not of the money, but of the value or benefits you can offer. *People want value, and they will pay you well for it.*

The Great One, the founder of the Persian religion of the Magi, Zoroaster, declared that doing good to others was not a duty, it was a joy, for it increased your own riches of mind and body.

To become rich you must find what it is you love to do, you must add great value, and you must find a way to leverage that greatness, as a simple lever can move a mighty boulder. Later Codes will tell you how to do that, but first had to come the Codes that ask you to think, to decide what is of value to you and what you want from life.

Should you choose to become rich in gold and silver, this is an honorable goal, provided the wisdom of this first Code is followed. Most of the unsurpassed riches of Persepolis were created in this way. These riches did not all come from tribute from conquered cities; much came as the accumulated wealth of the good people of this city.

Indeed, these are the very Codes I used to become the man many call the Richest Man in Persia.

The Core of Code 1:
The Quest for Real Riches.

1. To become rich, first you must give. No-one can become rich without enriching others. Abundance will be yours if you can help enough other people get what they want.

2. Do not think that money, or the quest for it, is evil. Money can do much good in the world, and possession of it has ruined fewer lives than the lack of it.

3. Riches must not come at the cost of happiness. Decide first that money wealth is what you truly want. There are many kinds of riches other than gold and silver. Do not sell your soul to buy your mansion.

4. Should you not plan wealth for the years ahead and for when you are no longer with your family to support them?

5. Stress kills as surely as a sword. Having money work hard for you is much more important that you working hard for money.

6. You will start to attract more money when you begin to think, not of the money, but of the value or benefits you can offer in exchange for it. If you think first of what you value and want out of life, you will begin to think of what others value and want.

Code 2: Master your Mind.

The world needs its dreamers. Dreams bring wondrous things within reach. They let us see what might be, and, having shown what might be, put a breeze under our wings to lift us.

If you have merely stumbled through life until now because you had nothing to aim for, look within yourself to find your dream.

Let it be clearly understood, if you do not have a dream of your own, and work towards it, you will be condemned to working all your life to fulfill someone else's dream.

Dreaming costs nothing. Not dreaming costs everything.

Dreams are our best nutrients for growth. All great achievers are dreamers. They see things others don't and reach for them. Dreams are the seeds from which realities grow - if they are nurtured by effort.

Dreams are the promise of what will one day be. Let dreams promise much for you.

Dream. Dream big. Let the size of your dream excite you and propel you into the step-by-step actions you need to take to make your dream come true.

It is said that the truly great harbor three major passions in their hearts:

1. *The need to give and receive love.*
2. *The quest for their destiny.*
3. *A true and deep empathy for the suffering of humanity.*

Let your dreams be big enough to embrace all three.

The masters have long known what is important in any plan for success in any field.

"Know yourself," said Socrates. Understand your desires, your needs, your strengths and weaknesses. Know what you value. The values you hold dear will determine the goals you are most likely to reach, and, when things go wrong, those same values will enable you to start again.

"Self-conquest is the greatest of victories," said Plato. And it is so.

Achievement comes through habits. Habits live in the mind and feed on whatever nutrients they find there. Let your values produce your nutrients.

It's very easy, yet very difficult, to become successful. All you have to do is fix in your mind the firm *intention* of becoming successful, then do everything you need to do, *today and every day*, until your actions become habits.

We all have bad habits, and they won't go away unless they are replaced by good habits. This takes persistent effort.

Striving for all achievement is hard. But what is harder - the effort of striving for success and wealth, or the result of not achieving them?

Remember the wisdom of the ancients: *you must accept either the pain of discipline or the pain of regret.*

If you truly desire wealth, commit yourself to doing whatever has to be done, within your ethical standards, to achieve it.

Never put a small value on yourself, because, rest assured, the world will not offer you a higher price. If you believe in yourself and in what you can do, nothing shall be impossible for you.

Birds fly because they *believe* they can fly.

Are you afraid of failure? Let it be known that the rich and successful people in life fail more than anyone else. Yes, the rich fail more, because they *try* more - but they are different. The rich keep trying until they succeed, and then the world forgets how often they failed.

Yes, you may fall over. Everyone falls. I, Tragoas, fell. But, if you fall seven times, lean on your values and rise seven times. You will fail on the road to success, but, no matter how many times you fail, *never be a failure*. Start again. Always. The greater the hardship, the greater the victory.

Dreams are drowned when the mind is swamped with doubt. Remember the old Persian proverb, "He who wants a rose must respect the thorn." Anticipate obstacles. It was not raining when Noah built the Ark. Prepare for trouble as best you can. But keep your mind on the rose. Remain positive.

And remember: *all glory comes from daring to begin*.

Think. Rich people think in order to grow rich. There can be no riches without thought. Pray to the Great God for wisdom. It is our greatest gift because it is the gift that allows us to choose well in life.

Never empty your heart to fill your purse. Always strive to do the right thing. Those who speak the truth are always at ease. Those with a clear conscience sleep well.

Desire is the first requirement for a person to attract wealth, but a wish to be rich, on its own, is of little avail. Goals must be specific to be tangible and therefore attainable. Goals can be increased, or changed, from time to time, and should be, but they must be specific and they should always fit within a time-frame.

You must know what you want, how much you want, and when you want it. You must be specific about how you plan to achieve your goals and what you are prepared to give up to achieve them.

Keep your goals simple and within reach, though you may have to stretch to reach them.

As knowledge and skills increase, so does the potential to earn - if you really know what you are aiming for.

To be great, you must dare to be great. The hunting is best where only the brave dare go. If you wish to change the world, or even your part of it, first change yourself. Dare to become the person you have to be. It is attitude that first determines success. If you would strengthen your abilities, first strengthen your thoughts.

Most people have no idea of where their money is going or the true state of their purse. They do not know what their true income or expenses are, nor do they know what their assets and liabilities are. To achieve riches, one must pay attention to these four things: *income, expenses, assets and liabilities.*

Let it be understood, there is not one single everyday item that does not contain the seeds of a great fortune. But you must think beyond the obvious. You must look for fresh ideas.

The way to ideas is through questions. Is there a new or different use for this item that lies unseen? Could this item be adapted and used in another way? The more questions you ask, the more ideas you will have. The more ideas you have, the more opportunities you'll have. Think.

Socrates was said to be the wisest man of his time. How did he become so? By asking questions.
If you master your own skills and talents and your own mind, you will also master your competitors. You already have five advantages over your competitors, provided that you take care of these advantages and hone them. They are:

1. *Your personal skills and knowledge.*
2. *The people you work with to create abundance.*
3. *Your own ways of marketing your services by adding value.*
4. *The strategies you develop to create wealth.*
5. *Your ethical standards and your ideals.*

The skills and knowledge you accumulate will become the bedrock of your success. The rich do not work harder than you do, they are no more intelligent, they just know more. And they are especially keen to learn and adopt the principles of creating wealth.

Always be willing to think and to learn. This is the way to minimize mistakes and maximize opportunities.

The people you learn from and the people you employ are your greatest assets. Having excellent merchandise or services is one thing, but, unless you have people who can create, produce and deliver these things to buyers, your efforts are wasted.

Be determined to find good people and keep them. Encourage them. Teach them about abundance and how to create it for themselves and others. Reward them, generously. Hire people with skills you don't have, or who are better than you. If you wish to be great, you must have great people.

Keep in mind always that the key to success is to create value for people and find ways of delivering this value to them. *The greater the value, the greater your success.*

And let it be clearly understood: thinking must not stop when you establish your business or whatever method you choose to create wealth. Thinking must be life-long. Plan the time and the quiet for it.

Count as one of your great treasures the sublime silence of early morning or deserted places, where you can rest your soul and find peace. Thinking is best done in serenity.

Always keep foremost in mind the special values you bring to your endeavors. Think habitually in terms of proper values and you will act in accordance with those values. *I, Tragoas, see no sense in having plenty to live on, and nothing to live for.*

Let it be known that the truly rich always have strong personal values. Values like passion, commitment, persistence and honesty. Such values set the truly rich apart and set the standards for themselves, for people who work with them, and for their search for abundance.

Those who are driven by their values give before they get in life. They are honest, fair and seek to understand others by listening. They strive to learn, even from their own mistakes, and look for opportunities in every problem. They accept responsibility for their actions. They always seek to do what is right.

The Core of Code 2: Master your Mind.

1. Dreaming costs nothing. Not dreaming costs everything. If you do not have a dream of your own, and work towards it, you will be condemned to working the rest of your life to fulfill someone else's dream. All great achievers are dreamers.

2. Know yourself. Think about your desires, your needs, your strengths and weaknesses. Know what you value. Your values will determine the goals you are most likely to reach, and, when things go wrong, will enable you to start again.

3. Achievement comes through habits. Fix in your mind the firm intention to become successful, then do everything you need to do, *today and every day*, until your actions become habits.

4. Striving for achievement is hard. But what is harder - the effort of striving for success, or the result of not achieving it? You must accept either the pain of discipline or the pain of regret. Commit yourself.

5. Are you afraid of failure? The rich fail more than anyone else, because they *try* more. They keep trying until they succeed. Be like the rich: no matter how many times you fail, *never become a failure*. Start again.

6. Goals must be tangible, and therefore attainable. They must be specific and set within a time-frame. Know what you want, how much you want, and when you want it. Plan to achieve your goals and what you are prepared to give, and give up, for them.

7. To be great, dare to be great. Be prepared to change, to become the person you have to be. Attitude determines success. Think. Look for ideas. Use your mind to master your skills and knowledge.

8. Always be willing to learn. Always seek to do what is right.

Code 3: Master Time.

Who controls your life? You or everyone else?

Unless you are one of the rare ones who have already mastered their time - and they are rare indeed - you must change the way you look at time, or be destined to mediocrity.

The ancients discovered important principles about time. Here are nine of them:

1. *The only day you have to do anything is today. Today is your most prized possession.*
2. *The mass of people think of how to <u>spend</u> their time. The wise think how to <u>use</u> it, and use it most effectively.*
3. *Patience and persistence can conquer the tyranny of time.*
4. *Do what has to be done, when it has to be done, whether you like it or not. Better yet, do it before it has to be done. This is especially true if something has to be done, but will cause distress or suffering. Do it anyway.*
5. *Begin the hardest or the longest task. Then persist.*

6. *Be prepared. Plan for tomorrow, then forget it. Tonight's plan is tomorrow's serenity.*
7. *Manage your time. Learn to say no. Learn to delegate. Control interruptions. Do the urgent and important things first.*
8. *Don't be busy, be effective. Perfection is a good goal, but not best practice. Settle for your best in the time you have. Promise less, give more.*
9. *Schedule time for you and your family first, and stick to it. This is your most important commitment.*

You may learn from yesterday, you may plan for tomorrow, but the only day you can live is today.

The sages of ancient India had this to say about today:

"Look to this day, for it is the life, the very life of life. In its brief course lie all the truths and realities of your existence: the bliss of growth, the glory of action, the splendor of beauty. For yesterday is but a dream, and tomorrow is only a vision. But today well lived makes every yesterday a dream of happiness and every tomorrow a vision of hope. Look well, therefore, to this day! Such is the salutation to the dawn!".

Today is the only time you have to do anything. Do what you can in it. Today is too precious to waste on mistakes and disappointments and might-have-beens. Today is the day for hope and expectation.

You don't have to solve all of life's problems *today*. But you can be happy *today*. You can strengthen your mind and learn something, *today*. You can talk softly, act courteously, do some good, *today*. You can defeat fear, *just for today*.

Today is the day to do what must be done, whether you like it or not, as well as you can. The greatest reward for today's effort is not what you get for it, but what you become by it.

Days come to you only one at a time, *and you never know how many you have left.* Can you afford to waste what the Great God sends you?

Let it be understood that nothing should be more highly prized than the value of each day. How high would you value this day if you knew it would be your last?

Those who have no goals in life think merely of how they shall *spend* their time. You, who wish to do better and to be better, should think of how you shall *use* it. Be careful how you use your time. Both work and leisure tend to expand so as to fill the time available for their completion. Limit your time for each task and save those precious hours.

Did not Socrates himself say that he is not only idle who does nothing, but he is idle who might be better employed?

You must use time to move wisely towards your goals and your destiny.

Ask yourself the question the masters ask: *what is the best thing I can do with my time right now?*

There will be a time to plan, a time to act; a time to plant, a time to reap; a time to work, a time for reward. There will be a time for haste, and a time for serenity. And there should always be time to pause and thank the Great God for all your blessings.

Sometimes great patience is required. If, in your quest for wealth, you invest your money to see it grow, you can use the power of compound returns, which puts time to use for your own benefit. The longer you leave your investments so that the returns on those investments are reinvested to earn more interest, the more certain will your fortune be. And the longer time goes, the faster your wealth grows

Patience and persistence outlast all other talents. Wherever you invest your hard-earned coins, manage your investment carefully and know the status of that investment at all times. But know that time is your greatest ally in your bid to grow your wealth. Let it work for you. Wait. Be patient. Your investment will grow as the value of property and money grows.

No great thing is created suddenly, any more than a bunch of grapes or a fig. If you tell me that you desire a fig, I answer that there must be time. Let the tree first blossom, then bear fruit, then let it ripen. Then you shall have figs aplenty.

Remember the old Persian proverb, "Patience is a bitter plant, but it has sweet fruit." As the Chinese people far to the north and west have always known, the mulberry leaf becomes a silk robe only with time and patience.

What you need is time to think, time to work, time to live, time to love. Time to give thanks. Time to become what you want to be. Time to give the world what you want to give.

Time is life's great uncertainty. May the Great God give you sufficient.

BRIAN MORGAN

The Core of Code 3: Master Time.

1. The ancients handed down nine important principles about time. I shall repeat a few of them here. Master them all.

2. You may learn from yesterday, you may plan for tomorrow, but the only day you can live is today. Today is the day for hope and expectation. Do your best in it.

3. Ask yourself: what is the best thing I can do with my time right now? Ask the same thing of tomorrow, of next week, of next year.

4. Patience and persistence outlast all other talents. They multiply the return on investments and make wealth grow. Time is needed to make anything great.

5. Perfection is a good goal, but not best practice. Do the best you can in the time you have. Don't promise the world. Promise less, and give more.

6. The greatest reward for today's effort is not what

you get for it, but what you become by it. Look to your values.

7. Schedule time for you and your family first. Let nothing get in the way of keeping that commitment.

8. Today is your most prized possession, but time is life's great uncertainty. You never know how many days you have left. Can you afford to waste even one?

Code 4:
Cast off your Rags.

Many are the poor who live in squalor outside the walls of Persepolis, and many are those who will join them after Alexander brings this city to its knees. How can such people break out of the trap of misery and lift their sights to the abundance that truly awaits them? Is such a wonder possible?

I have learned for myself that such a thing <u>is</u> possible. Was I not numbered among the poor myself - and ashamed before my family and my friends?

This much I, Tragoas, know to be true: *To lift your spirit and your mind to dream of new beginnings, you have the wisdom of the ancients to support you.*

This is why I hasten to record these Codes, so that such wisdom will never be lost. For is not wisdom itself a treasure of infinite value? If a fortune is made and a fortune lost, will not the wisdom of the ages restore it - if that wisdom be applied? My testimony is proof of it.

Most people will earn much money in their lifetimes, yet they can only dream of the joys it can bring, for money slips through the fingers like water from the stream. All about them there is wealth to be seen and wealth to be earned, but they manage to keep little of it for themselves. Why is it that people cannot acquire more money than they need for food, clothing and a roof over their heads?

It is not how much income you earn that matters, but how much of it you keep and how long that money works for you. For some people, the more they earn, the more they spend.

But, from dawn to dark, people work, and they work well, hoping that one day the Great God will smile upon them and make them wealthy. But the God does not make men wealthy. Only men can do this.

The Babylonians showed us that the reason most people never grow rich is that they never seek to do so. They work hard and long at the work they have chosen to do and they give that work their best efforts. One will work hard at the forge, another on the caravans, yet another at the market, and another as a minstrel. At that work they succeed. They become skilled at what they try to do. If they chose instead to become rich, then they may have succeeded at that.

Let it be known: *It is better to overcome poverty than to succumb to it - but the desire and the determination must be great.*

Think of each gold coin as a money seed that you must grow into a mighty money tree. Destroy an acorn and the oak tree cannot be. Squander your money and your hope for the future dies. Let it be known that undisciplined man is the only animal whose desires multiply faster than they can be satisfied. Fool that he is, he always ignores what he should do and gives in to what pleases him. He does what he *wants* to do, rather than what he *ought* to do.

Ignorance about managing money can mean losing in a few minutes what it takes a year to earn. Many people struggle because whenever they earn more money, they spend more. Even worse, they borrow more and this debt carries an interest burden that can be both heavy and life-long.

The more people you owe money to, the poorer you are. Many are in debt, but the debt must never get out of balance. If you have too much debt, you can lose everything you have - your family, your work, your home, your self-esteem, everything.

Debt should never be used to purchase items that will fall in value, unless they are essential. Debt preferably should always be used for assets that will grow in value.

But what should you do if you find yourself locked in the dungeon of debt? The best way to eliminate debt is to pay off one debt and then apply that extra payment to another debt in a progression.

Paying off debts is an excellent investment because you are paying more interest for that debt than you would normally earn investing with the money lenders.

How do you start to save? Coins hidden under your bed are better than nothing, but putting those coins to work earning more coins will build your fortune. In addition, you will be forging a habit of saving that will serve you well for all of your days. Some habits are good and are smiled upon by the God.

The beginning, according to Plato, is half the whole business. You must do what you can, with what you have, where you are. No matter how small the start. Then you can grow.

If you save money by giving it to the money lender to use, this is a good start to your first income stream, but what you are doing is making the money lender rich. If you wish to be rich yourself, you must stop letting others use your money and become like the money lender yourself. You must use other people's money at a price low enough that you can produce more than you have had to pay for it. I will speak more of this later, but you must aim to create income streams that flow whether you work or cast a net fishing on the river bank.

Money in the future will be controlled by the same rules that controlled it in the days when

Persepolis was rich and free. The Codes will always be true.

When poor people wish to become rich they must possess three qualities:

1. They must have a clear and vivid dream for the future and a plan to get there.
2. They must believe in delaying their pleasures in life and act on that belief.
3. They must use the power of leverage.

I will speak more of these qualities in these Codes.

You must learn to pay yourself first. This is the power of self discipline. It is the great secret given to the world by the Babylonians. If you cannot control yourself, there is no point in gaining riches. The more you gain, the more you will spend and the more miserable you will become. If you do not pay yourself from what you earn, how are you different from the slaves, who, at the mercy of their masters, toil all their lives for food, water and a bed at night?

Surely the most basic idea of money is that a part of all your earnings, whether you earn little or much, is yours to keep? The Babylonians asked: why should you work for everyone else and not for yourself? You pay the boot-maker, you pay the food merchant, you pay for the roof over your head, you pay the garment-maker, but what do you have to show for what you have earned after spending on these things? You have paid everyone but yourself. You are a slave to everybody.

Wealth cannot be measured by the size of the purse that carries it. The purse quickly empties if there is no stream of coins to refill it. Income - and streams of it - that is the secret.

To take your first steps on the road to riches, and before you can think of becoming a money lender yourself, you may lend small sums to the money lender and increase this amount at regular intervals. The interest which the money lender adds to your investment will increase your wealth and the money this interest earns will further increase it.

If a man saves 100 coppers and gives it to the money lender to keep for 50 years at a rental of one fourth of its value every four years, and lets that rental be added each year to the 100 coins invested, how much will he have at the end of 50 years? Some might say about 400 coppers, the original 100 coins, plus the rental earned, but they would be wrong. Because the rental has earned interest, and that interest has earned interest and so on for 50 years, the man will receive back 1670 coppers for his investment. His money has multiplied almost 17 times while he did nothing but wait. *Such is the magic of compounding.*

There are many kinds of work at which people may earn their first coins. Each of these create a stream of money and the laborer may keep part of that stream for his own use. The size of the stream depends on the ability of the worker. Any honest labor produces the first of your income streams. Such an income stream may not always flow as reliably as it has in the past. Will not our walls be under siege, even as the scribes complete these Codes? But a person willing to work can always bounce back and get that income steam flowing again.

And whenever that stream is flowing, let the full stream flow into your purse, but let no more than nine-tenths flow out again. If you do that, will not your purse soon be full to overflowing so that you must rent it to the money lender to make it work for you?

This is a simple plan, but the truth is always simple. Do not underestimate, as most of the citizens do, the strength of this plan because of its simplicity. This rule, faithfully followed, will make all other Codes easier.

Wealth increases fast when earnings are put to good use. When every coin earns more money for you, your worth increases rapidly and the earnings themselves increase that flow of wealth, provided that you invest those earnings instead of spending them. So keep for yourself part of everything you earn for the rest of your life. Make it one tenth at least, never less. And make it work for you.

Rich people know they can achieve success if they hold a dream for the long term. They are willing to sacrifice now in order to gain later. And they make their money earn money and that earned money earn more money. *That is what they call the power of compounding*.

Pay yourself first and all others afterwards. Every piece of gold you keep for yourself must become your slave. Put it to work to earn coppers. And put those coppers to work to earn still more. Thus will your savings compound and multiply. There is a magic in compounding that many, even kings, do not understand.

I say it again, for this is the foundation upon which your fortune will be built: Pay yourself first - then spend what you *need* to spend on rent for the roof over your head, on food and others in need and on penance to the God. And then, and only then, pay the raiment-maker and sandal-maker and the jewelry-merchant for the things you *want*.

If you kept for yourself one tenth of everything you earned, how much would you have in ten years? The answer is not the amount you earn in one year, it is more than that. If every gold daric you put aside is put to work for you, it will earn interest and, if that interest is put to work, it can earn more interest. *That is the power of compounding and the way to riches*. I repeat it because, unless you use this power, you will never become rich.

True wealth is like a tree, it grows from a seed. And the first coin you save from your earnings is the seed from which your money tree will grow. Plant that seed as soon as you can and plant others and plant the interest that comes from those seeds and watch your wealth grow.

When you do put aside one tenth of everything you earn, a strange thing will happen. You will find that you still have enough money to live on, even though you were struggling to manage before. You will find that you can live on nine-tenths of your earnings as well as you can on all of your earnings, because you are thinking of your *needs* first, and putting aside those things you desire, but cannot afford, out of the nine-tenths.

Expenses, if uncontrolled, expand to the size of your income, and very often more. This is the road to financial stress, poverty and ruin. In a room full of people, all will be earning different incomes. They will have different needs, different families, different responsibilities - yet all will have the same empty purse. They spend money according to its availability. Desires grow wherever people believe they can be gratified.

Should you live to work, or work to live? What are your goals in life? Are you working for those goals, or the goals of everybody else?

Aristotle, the teacher of Alexander, said that the multitudes constantly seek pleasure and a life of gratification. This, he said, makes them little more than slaves, for the life they seek is a life for grazing animals.

Delay that gratification; seek only what is needed. Such is the way to wealth and true happiness. You must learn to delay satisfaction and enjoy the sense of anticipation. The difference between your needs and wants will not cause you discomfort. In the years to come, there will be great satisfaction from this self-discipline.

Do not confuse what you need with what you want. Everyone wants more than their income can satisfy. Spend all your income and the things you want will still be wanted. Everyone is weighed down with things they want, things they cannot gratify. Spend your money on the things that are necessary and other things that are possible through spending only nine-tenths of your income. Consider all additional things that you want as things that must be delayed. Forget them.

A need is something that is necessary for survival or a reasonable quality of life. A want is something that provides convenience or pleasure.

Wants come at great cost and provide the appearance of wealth, but they take you farther away from it. How much of your house is for you and how much is for impressing others? How much of your chariot is for you and how much for others to see? What is sufficient? What is enough? How much of your income is wasted pursuing the life you want rather than the life you need?

There is no need to restrict yourself to a severe lifestyle. You do not have to become as the ascetics of India. Few can stick to such a plan, and why should you? Do not eliminate from your life those things you really need, but restrain yourself.

Use the wisdom of Aristotle, the wisdom of the ages. The wisdom that can be yours.

BRIAN MORGAN

The Core of Code 4:
Cast off your Rags.

1. It is possible to break out of the trap of poverty and misery and shame, and to lift your sights to the abundance that awaits you. Let the wisdom of the ancients show you the way.

2. It is not how much income you *earn* that matters most, but how much of it you *keep*. It is easier to overcome poverty than to succumb to it, but the desire and the determination must be great.

3. Debt can work for you, or it can destroy you. It should never be used to purchase that which will fall in value, unless it is essential to do so. Use debt to purchase assets that will grow in value.

4. To eliminate debt, pay off one debt as quickly as possible, then apply that extra payment to the next debt in a progression. Since money costs more to borrow from the money lenders than they pay you to invest with them, paying off debt is, in itself, an excellent investment in your future.

5. Begin saving by investing what money you can with the money lenders. Let these coins earn more coins, and let those coins be invested to earn even more. As wealth grows, seek other safe investments that return more. But always invest the profits you make. Squandering them will squander your future wealth.

6. When you find safe investments that return more, you can then borrow money to invest because your returns on your investments will exceed what you have to pay the money lenders.

7. The great secret of the Babylonians was to pay yourself first from all your earnings. Do this even when you are rich. Pay yourself at least one coin from every 10 you earn. Invest this money and reinvest the profits. This is the first giant step towards riches.

8. Delay gratification. Control your expenses. Spend on what you need, not on what you want. Gratification destroys abundance.

Code 5:
A World of Abundance.

It is a simple matter for anyone to become wealthy within their lifetime. If one gold coin were put to use every day so that it returns one gold coin each year for every 10 invested, and those gold coins were also invested, those gold coins would grow to one million gold coins in just 56 years. If one gold coin continued to be invested for another 10 years, at the end of that period 2,700,000 gold coins will have accumulated.

Anyone can thus earn riches over a period of time. To become rich faster, invest more money or find ways to make the money grow faster.

Our brothers in India to the east long ago said: "Out of abundance came abundance and still abundance remained." The world is full of abundance. The only shortage is in the minds of those who cannot see it. Abundance awaits all who apply the principles of acquiring it.

I will say that again: *there is an abundance of money, but some simple rules must be obeyed.*

Those who have merely survived in the years they have been working have struggled because either they have failed to learn the rules that govern riches or else they have not followed those rules. If people discover the rules for accumulating riches and make this their task and do it well, then riches will follow.

But, you say, if becoming rich was so simple and if everyone did it, surely there would be not enough riches for everyone? But I say to you that *wealth grows wherever people work.* If a worker gives productive value in exchange for his earnings, has he not doubled the value of those earnings? He and the person who employs him both have value, do they not?

If a stone-polisher works on a rough gemstone and thus increases its value, has he not created value? *All effort that produces an increase in value contributes to abundance.* Gold in the ground has no value. But, if workers mine it and cart it to the market and sell it, then it has value and it contributes to abundance. If a jeweler buys that gold and fashions jewelry from it, does he not increase value, and also contribute to abundance? When the jeweler collects coins for the jewelry, he has the value in coins and his buyer has the value in jewelry. Has not money multiplied?

If a merchant were to build a new shop, is the money he paid for it gone? No, the builder has part of it and his laborers have part of it, those who supplied the building materials have part of it and the one who designed the shop has part of it. Everyone who works on that shop has part of the money, yet when the shop is finished is it not worth all the money that was invested in it? In fact it is worth *more* because the land upon which it stands is worth more. In addition, the land that adjoins it is worth more because the shop has increased the value of the area. The same magical thing happens when you build a house.

Riches grow in ways beyond most people's comprehension. There is no limit to it. Abundance is there for everyone.

And you can create abundance by using the principles of Code 4: when your savings start to earn interest, should you spend that interest on wine and fine robes? No, that interest should be put into your investment with your original coins so that you can earn more. First, start to live on less than you earn. Next, take advice from those experienced enough to give it, and make your money and its earnings work for you. Thus you will know how to acquire money, how to keep it and how to use it.

But be sure that advice comes from those capable of true counsel in the knowledge you seek.

The wise one, Plato, once said, "Everything that deceives may be said to enchant." There would be no deception if we could see at a glance the deceit for what it was. Look deeper. Expect danger. Look to the person who is giving advice. If the person is not genuine, his offer cannot be genuine.

The ancients have decreed that there are four sides to wealth:

1. *What you earn. Your income.*
2. *What you spend. Your expenses.*
3. *What you own. Your assets.*
4. *What you owe. Your liabilities.*

The rich develop the habit of working only towards assets and the income that can be gained from them. Luck has little to do with success. Remember the Persian proverb, "Luck is infatuated with the efficient." Luck is a sheep. It blindly follows planning and work.

You must learn the difference between an asset and a liability. An asset is something that creates income and long-term profit. A liability is something that consumes income. To become rich you need to accumulate assets and only accumulate liabilities that help you do so. It is important to buy real assets, not assets that are consumed or decline in value. You are truly wealthy when your assets generate enough income to meet your living expenses with a surplus to continue to reinvest in assets. You cannot do this without creating abundance along the way, both for yourself and for others with whom you deal.

Assets fall into different types. These include businesses that do not require your presence, income-generating property, taking a share of someone else's business that earns income, taking payment for the use of your thoughts and ideas, and anything else that has value and produces income.

You must first learn to guard your money from loss. Do not be tempted by those who say you can make large amounts by investment in their projects. High interest comes at high risk. The first rule of investment is to secure your investment principal. Should large earnings be sought when the principal may be lost? Before you entrust your money in any venture, learn about the dangers that may lie ahead.

Protect your money by investing it where it is safe, where it can be reclaimed if needed, and where you will earn fair interest.

There are four basic ways of making money and contributing to abundance:

1. *Work for someone else. This is how most of us start, at least, and, using the methods of the Babylonians, you can create value and gradually become rich this way.*

2. *Work for yourself. This is usually a better, faster way to wealth, and you can help others become rich along the way. But beware: the more successful you become, the harder you will work.*
3. *Invest your money in businesses owned by others, or ventures or valuables or property - assets you expect to grow in value or produce income. This is an even better way, a more sure way and, often, a fast way to create abundance.*
4. *Create a business of your own that you can replicate. This can be an absolutely wondrous way to accumulate wealth and create abundance.*

Everything around you began as a thought in someone's mind. The chariot you drive. The bench you sit on. The tools you work with. If you can think of something useful and create it, you are on the road to riches and you will be creating abundance.

For the student of riches, there are three things you need:

1. *The right thought or idea.*
2. *The will to do what is necessary.*
3. *The people who can do for you what you cannot do yourself.*

You must determine what service, product, or information you will offer in return for riches. You must be determined to offer such things in the quantity and quality necessary to gain riches. And you must gather around you the people necessary to help you achieve those riches.

There is a world of abundance waiting for you to decide how to gather some of it for yourself. But be aware: unless you are prepared to create abundance for others, you will not truly gather it for yourself. This is the law discovered by the ancients and proved by every generation since.

BRIAN MORGAN

The Core of Code 5:
A World of Abundance.

1. The world is full of abundance. The only shortage is in the minds of those who cannot see it. Abundance awaits all who apply the principles of acquiring it.

2. Wealth grows wherever people work and create value. If you give productive value equivalent to your earnings in exchange for them, have you not created abundance? Do not both you and the person who employs you have value? If a jeweler sells in the marketplace, does he not create abundance? Does he not have the value of the jewelry in coins, while the buyer has the value in the jewelry itself?

3. If you build a house, is the money you paid for it gone? No, the builder, the laborers, the suppliers, the designer all have their share of it, yet the house is still worth all that money to you. In fact, it is worth more, because the land upon which it stands is now worth more. In addition, adjoining

properties have also risen in value. Is not abundance created, then, whenever you buy an asset that grows in value?

4. Those who use the principles of Code 4 create abundance. If they invest savings to earn interest, and if they reinvest the coins they make to earn more, they are creating wealth and creating abundance.

5. To become rich, you need to accumulate assets that produce income, and only accumulate liabilities, or debt, that helps you do so. In doing so, you will create abundance for yourself and for those with whom you deal.

6. The four basic ways of earning income and creating abundance are to work for others, to work for yourself, to invest your money and to create a business. In addition, if you can think of something useful and create it, you will be on the road to riches and will be creating abundance.

7. Only by creating abundance for others can you truly gather it for yourself.

Code 6:
No-one Becomes Rich Alone.

The heritage of the past is the seed that brings forth the harvest of the future. Man will always stand in need of man. And no-one should ever be alone.

Find the right people to work for you and with you. Seek people who will help you achieve your dreams, and you will help them achieve theirs.

Search out a master who has tackled your mountain before you. Find the people who will join together to help you achieve more goals easier and faster. Each of these people will know other people and these other people will know still more people. Through these contacts you will have many ways of reaching people in your quest for riches.

Link up with others who already deal with the kinds of people you wish to deal with. In all of these groups of people there are several very important people, those who already have large groups of people that they deal with. These people can make wondrous things happen if you find a way to join your efforts with theirs.

It is important to find a master or counselor when starting a business. A master is someone who has already achieved what you want to do and has been successful at doing it. Do not look for an advisor who wants to tell you how to do things, but has not personally done those things.

The world is full of experts. Beware. Advice is plentiful and freely given away, but the wise take only that which is worthy of the taking.

Many people are hurt badly when highly paid counselors hand out investment advice. They are hurt because many of these people giving advice have no experience in the matter in which they offer advice. Always seek advice from those who have experience in the area you seek advice. If you wish to know about building, talk to a builder. If you wish to know about goats, talk to one who herds goats. If you wish to know about the law, speak to one who counsels in the law. Advice is only worth receiving if it is given by a person of experience.

Seek the wisdom of those experienced in investing their own money for profit. Such knowledge is worth more than the gold itself because, if you had gold and lost it, more can always be earned to start investing again. *Wisdom is worth more than gold*.

Those experienced in investing money can protect your wealth from risk. If all your earnings were in your purse, you would guard that purse with your life, would you not? Be aware that those who are entrusted with your money will not guard it with their lives. But those with experience in the type of investment you seek will ensure the risk of loss is small. Their livelihood depends upon it.

Who can name the price of experience? It is often bought with the price of all that a man has. Have not men lost their homes, their wives, their children and had nothing to show but the experience of their misfortune? If a master, who has paid the price for his experience, can give it to you for nothing but your time, would you not be a fool to turn your back on such a gift? And even if he asked for coins in return for his knowledge, would not the cost be cheap?

Socrates taught Plato. Plato taught Aristotle. Aristotle taught Alexander the Macedonian.

All great achievers once listened at the feet of a master and thus learned the steps to wisdom and self-mastery. With these skills, the ordinary become extraordinary and begin to accumulate riches of all kinds.

Always take people with you on your great journey into the future. Show your workers how to share your vision in a number of ways:

1. *Help them to fulfill their own vision while*

becoming part of yours. Help them see it.
2. *Show them how your business works, how things are done in your unique way, what is expected of them. Give them a challenge they can rise to.*
3. *Urge people to share in the exhilaration of success and reward them as you, and they, succeed.*
4. *Insist that you and they share and accept responsibility for future success. This will help their self-esteem.*
5. *Make your workplace as stress-free as possible and the workload as enjoyable as possible. People must have time and incentive to dream their own dreams.*
6. *Prepare them for the struggles ahead and celebrate their victories, even the small ones.*
7. *Demonstrate often that you care for your people and appreciate what they do. Show your respect for them as human beings doing honorable work to benefit their families.*
8. *Constantly share with them your vision for the future, yours and theirs. Help them believe in something bigger than themselves. Show them how important they are in this vision and what their rewards might be.*

Let it be known and understood: *you cannot buy respect, you must earn it*. You do this by never asking someone to do something your conscience would not allow you to do yourself.

The ancients have made it clear: you must have loyalty to people though they are not perfect; you must have faith that they will stick to you as you stick to them; you must have hope that shared joy will outweigh shared disappointments; and your must have patience enough to outlive betrayals and setbacks.

People are human, they are not gods. Do not expect more from them than they are capable of giving. But, if you treat them with respect and dignity, they will give you more than you expect.

Let the kings build walls to keep people apart. You must build bridges to bring people together.

BRIAN MORGAN

The Core of Code 6:
No-one Becomes Rich Alone.

1. Find the right people to work for you and with you. Such people will help you achieve your dreams, and you will help them achieve theirs.

2. Search out a master who has tackled your mountain before you, someone who has been successful and is willing to share experience with you. Such advice can make a fortune and avoid much pain. Wisdom is worth more than gold.

3. Beware of self-proclaimed experts. Advice is plentiful, but the wise take only that which is worthy of the taking. Be sure the advisor has experience and success in the area you seek advice. If you seek investment advice, seek out those with experience in the type of investment you chose.

4. All great achievers once listened at the feet of a master and thus learned the steps to wisdom and self-mastery. With these skills, the ordinary become extraordinary and begin to accumulate riches of all kinds.

5. If you employ workers, share your vision with them. Show them what is expected of them. Stretch them. Give them responsibility and rewards. Care for them and respect them. Help them to believe in something bigger than themselves. Be loyal to them, always.

Code 7:
The Power of Leverage.

A lever makes heavy work light. If you wish to create wealth, you must use a big lever.

If you create a product *once* that is purchased by *many* people, that is leverage. If you then find *another use* for that product so that even more people use it, that is greater leverage. Leverage creates many income streams not only for you, but for all those merchants or other people who distribute your product.

Borrowing money creates leverage, as we shall see.

Another form of leverage is *other people's knowledge*. It may take too long to gain the necessary knowledge for yourself, so you can learn from others. The very best way to do this is to find a master who will teach you the ways to wealth. You can learn all they know and do all that they do to earn riches. One simple idea might save you 10 years of effort.

Leverage, therefore, is also about *maximizing results in a minimum amount of time.*

Another use of leverage is to use *other people's ideas*. It will pay handsomely to associate with those who can share with you ideas for gaining riches. You will recall that I, Tragoas, was greatly rewarded by encouraging others to produce ideas for my business, and I rewarded them.

Another lever is the use of *other people's time*. Some people will freely give you their time, others will sell you their time. With that time comes their knowledge, their skills, their talent and all the other resources that will help you become rich. Time must be leveraged to multiply success.

If your skills earn you one daric per hour in the marketplace, and you work 10 hours per day, you can earn 10 darics per day. But what if you taught less skilled workers to do what you do? They might be happy to earn half a daric per hour, or five darics per day. You would then earn five darics per day for yourself, and yet you have spent no time at all in the marketplace.

If the systems and procedures you set up to do this worked, what is to stop you employing five or 10 or 20 workers to do the same thing? Would you not be creating abundance for these workers, and also for yourself? If you had five workers, you would earn 25 darics. If you had 20, you would earn 100. And all this time you might be sitting by the river casting for fish.

Selling your own time in the marketplace will never make you rich, as I found in my early days. However, selling other people's time at a profit can create abundance and make you rich. And the richer you become, the more good you can do in the world.

Let it be clearly understood: *you should do only those things that only you can do, and you should develop systems and procedures that allow others to do everything else.*

Using *other people's work* as leverage creates abundance. Everyone needs to work. They need to eat, they need a roof over their heads. Hire these people and give them the tasks that you do not want to do or should not do or cannot do as well as they can. Once your investment has been started, it should operate without any effort on your part. Have others do whatever needs to be done to keep that income stream flowing.

You will recall my Circle of Counselors and the workers who responded to my generosity by doing more than was asked of them. Leverage such as this is available to you.

As a sage once said: *the creation of a thousand trees begins with one tiny seed.*

Leverage is the power to control much with little. We have seen several kinds of leverage.

Another is the use of *other people's money*. If you borrow money to purchase a house, you may need one tenth of the value of the house as your contribution and borrow the rest, and yet you control *all* of the property.

Borrowing money creates leverage. If you use 1000 gold darics of your money and borrow the rest to purchase a house for 10,000 gold coins, that house might increase in value by 1000 gold coins in one year. That is a good, but not unusual return on an investment of 10,000 coins in property. However, leverage allows your 1000 gold coins to profit on the full 10,000 gold coins, so that your 1000 investment has earned *you* the 1000 gold coins in just one year. The money lender receives only his interest from this profit. You receive the rest.

The way to get rich is to use other people's money in such a way that you make more than what you had to pay to borrow it.

What are the secrets of the money lenders? Can you profit from their experience?

They will tell you that the safest loans they make are to those whose assets are of more value than the thing they wish to purchase. They own property or jewels or herds or other things which could be sold to repay the debt. The money lenders are thus assured that the loan will be repaid because the loan is secured by property or other assets.

The money lenders also will lend to those who have the capacity to repay and to repay on time. Such loans are based on the principles of work and honesty. There are those who have neither assets nor the ability to earn regular coins. For these people the money lenders will not lend or, if they do, they will charge high interest because of the high risk they take in lending to them. Such people may be good and honest, but if they are unable to repay the money lender, why should he lend to them? Would you?

The money lender will also consider the attitude of the person seeking to borrow. The lenders will listen to a sound plan for the use of the money and its repayment, but they will consider too risky the person who demonstrates great emotions rather than a sound plan.

Nor will they lend money to those who wish to borrow because of their own mistakes. Lenders are not keen to lend to those who wish to repay other loans with the money.

The money lender will also be cautious about youth and the desire of youth to earn wealth quickly. Fast wealth often means high risk and why should the money lender accept such risk? Understand that hopeless debt is a burden of great sorrow and regret. Money lenders are in the business of lending money, they encourage it. But they recommend it for a wise purpose. They do not wish to accept the risk for your rash decisions.

Better that the money lender and you be cautious at the start than both of you regret your decision at the end.

Loans used to finance something that depreciates or is consumed are usually bad loans. A loan for your chariot therefore might be considered a bad loan because your chariot depreciates in value as it gets older. However, if you use your chariot to produce income or it is a necessary part of your life, then the debt is a necessary one and no longer bad.

Debt for items that are consumed or depreciate are expensive (they carry high interest rates), they are unproductive because they are used for things that depreciate instead of assets that appreciate in value, and they are a last resort type of debt. High interest paid to fund your extravagant lifestyle means considerably less money for you to invest in assets that grow.

A good loan, on the other hand, is one that serves a definite financial purpose and to purchase an asset that will grow in value and return good income.

Your home will prove to be an excellent asset that appreciates greatly. The loan for it is good because it allows you to provide security for your family, but also allows you to own an appreciating asset. It is highly regarded by the money lenders and is therefore the cheapest of all loans. It is highly flexible because you can pay it off over a very long time and the money lender will usually give you many options. Using your home as security, you can borrow to invest in assets that will produce income or grow wealth, or both. It is the cheapest form of lending. It is a loan that can be applied to produce income or to grow wealth.

Loans used for buying a home or a business or an investment are good loans provided that the return on your investments exceeds the cost of the loan. And provided that you take care to guard your principal from loss.

Do not spend more on your home than you should. How much home should you have? The money lenders will tell you that the debt you carry should be no more than a reasonable portion of the income you produce.

You should consider and regularly review your net worth. This is your financial assets minus your financial liabilities. It is what you are worth after paying off all your debt. It is your real worth.

Always know what that worth is.

These are the secrets of the money lenders. Have them in mind when you apply to borrow, and, should the opportunity present itself, put these principles to use to lend to others only as the wise lend, and to create additional income streams for yourself.

Once you have established a success in any endeavor, why not use the knowledge you have gained to build a similar success, or one in another city? Or why not add to your income streams by adding more goods or services to increase that success?

Do not sit on your heels. Leverage success.

The Core of Code 7: The Power of Leverage.

1. A lever creates much from little. If you create a product that is purchased by *many*, that is leverage. If you can find *another use* for it, so that even more use it, that is leverage. Leverage can help create many streams of income.

2. You can use *other people's knowledge* as a lever to achieve. This is the value of a master. One new skill may save years of effort, or save you from disaster.

3. *Other people's ideas* can be used as leverage. Encourage others to find ideas that will solve your problems or create opportunities, then reward them for it.

4. You can leverage *other people's time and effort*. As you have seen from my testimony, this can multiply success and create abundance, for you and others. Do only those things that only you can do, and allow others to do everything else. I shall speak more of this later.

5. You can use *other people's money* as a lever. Debt can be used to purchase income-producing assets, including property. The way to get rich is to use debt in such a way that you make more with it than you had to pay to borrow it.

6. Study *the secrets of the money lenders*. You will then know how to borrow and how to lend. You will learn how to avoid high risk and you will understand the sorrow and regret unwise debt can cause. Caution when borrowing can avoid much regret and misery. The secrets of the money lenders will teach you when to borrow and when to avoid debt. Money is a great lever, if you know its secrets.

7. Regularly review your net worth, your assets minus your debt. Always be aware of that net worth.

8. When you establish success in any field, multiply it. Leverage success.

Code 8:
Many Streams of Income.

There are many who will advise you to invest all the money you have in one place, and then watch it as carefully as the eagle watches her nest. I, Tragoas, say that advice is bad advice.

Sometimes such a strategy might work, and *sometimes* it can make you very rich. But sometimes it does not work, and, when it doesn't, you *always* end up poor, because everything you have is gone.

Let it be known that the ancients advise the very opposite strategy.

Far away to the north many small streams trickle out of the mountains and surge down to gradually link with one another and form the mighty surging Euphrates and Tigris rivers. In such a way, you must aim to create many streams of income to create your wealth.

If one income stream goes dry, it will not slow the flow of your river because the other streams will continue to flow. Such was the advice given to me by my father and his friend, Ramazan. Fortunately, I followed that advice.

You have seen in my testimony how I was betrayed and robbed and thrown onto the scrapheap of despair. All, I thought, was lost. But it was not so. Some of my income streams were still flowing, others could be made to flow again with little effort.

Many income streams not only saved me and my family, they also allowed the money lenders to get back the money I owed them, and allowed by suppliers to be paid for their services. Even more important, they allowed my workers to keep working, thus enabling them to feed their families.

When other people become involved in your quest for wealth, you have a responsibility to them to succeed. The greater the number of people and the greater their dependency on you, the greater your responsibility.

You owe it to them, as well as yourself, to keep moving towards success, no matter what circumstances confront you. And the best way to ensure this is to have many income streams flowing into your river of wealth.

When you are able to do this, you should even plan for the contingency that you will not be there to keep those income streams flowing. Streams of income should be made to flow whether you are present or not. This means that the money you earn for investing your money should itself earn money. *You must aim to have money working for you instead of you working for money.*

How do you start your income streams?

We have seen that you start with the work you are employed to do by others. You invest with the money lenders at least one gold daric in every 10 you earn. As these gold coins earn you silver coins or coppers, your first stream has started to trickle. When you reinvest those profits to also earn money, the flow increases. This is the Babylonian way to gradual, but sure wealth, provided you have the discipline.

Then you seek additional streams by *finding needs you can fill*, either yourself in your spare time, or by the efforts of others. Look for merchandise or services that will fulfill needs. You can do as I did, and *bring buyers and sellers together* with little cost on your part.

Let several things be clearly understood:

1. *Wherever there is a need, the merchandise or service can be found to fill it.*
2. *You must seek to add value to everything you do and to be unique, because this is the way to attract money from buyers to your income streams.*
3. *You must invite others to watch for opportunities that will create income streams for you, and rewards for themselves.*

The rich, as we have seen, purchase assets that grow in value and generate income streams. These assets can be businesses, investments, services or ideas. And there is one critical element that separates the truly wealthy from the rest. It is that extra income is created by buying assets with their surplus income. They do not waste surplus income on unnecessary desires soon forgotten.

At every step along your road to wealth, be aware that undisciplined spending eats abundance, puts wealth out of reach, and dries up income streams.

Yes, income streams can come from many things. You can invest in other businesses, you can buy your own house, you can buy other houses, you can show other people how to create wealth, you can find a product or service that will fill a need.

Then ask yourself: Is the product or service you have selected practical? Is it what people need now? Does it serve a basic human need? What is the growth potential of this product or service? Will it work now or will it take years of hard work? Never be afraid to ask people to find the answers to such questions, because your success depends on the right answers.

Thus you increase your streams of income, but do not do so recklessly. A fool and his purse soon part company. Test each stream before you seek a full flow, and *only move on to another stream when the last one is flowing freely and surely.*

We have seen that there are four basic ways of making money. *You can work for someone else, you can work for yourself, you can own a business, or you can be an investor.* But, whatever methods you chose, you must follow the rules for success, or your income streams will run dry.

If you decide to work for yourself rather than develop a business that works for you, this can be the most rewarding of work, but also the most risky. Self employment is the hardest kind of work and the failure rates are high. Sometimes being a success can be worse than failing because being a success means working harder than if you were employed by someone else. The longer your success lasts, and the greater it is, the harder you have to work, because *you* are vital to everything that happens.

Very often people who work for themselves use life savings or borrow money to start that self employment and, after years of struggle and hard work, they have no business and no life savings and sometimes even a debt to pay off. Nine out of 10 of self-employed people fail within five years. Of those that remain, nine out of 10 fail in the next five years. Almost all small businesses operated by self-employed people disappear within 10 years.

But this need not be, if the principles in these Codes are followed.

To multiply money faster, there are two things you can do. You can use *leverage,* which often means debt, or you can invest in assets that produce high rates of return. The lure of big interest always entails big risk. Always. If it did not, you would be knocked over by the hordes stampeding to get to it before you. The world is full of silver tongues.

I say again: *Big returns mean big risk.* It is better to have debt to purchase an asset with lower risk than to risk all you have on something you know in your heart is too good to be true. The first rule of investment must always be *security for your principal.* No matter where you invest, learn the dangers first. Probe. Ask questions. Invest only where your hard-earned principal may be readily reclaimed.

However, there is also a risk with debt, for even a low-risk investment can go wrong. *That is why it is so important to have multiple streams of income coming into your river of wealth.*

There are always ways of gaining extra income to invest. You can rent out a room in your home, you can sell your skills and talents to neighbors and friends, you can take the thing you enjoy doing and make of it a small business, or as we shall see, a *niche* business.

Many people try to do what the rich do and have what the rich have, and they go into debt to do so. That is not what the rich do. The rich are content with little, while the money they borrow earns more money streams for them. When those money streams gather into a mighty river, then they can buy the grand chariot or the bigger house.

In creating multiple streams of income, use as little money of your own as possible. Use leverage. This will lower your risk and your goal should be to be risk-free income.

Look to the river. If only one stream flows into it, and that stream runs dry, there *is* no river. If there is no river, those who depend on its life-giving waters face desperate times. If, however, many streams flow into the river, and one dries up, the river still flows, and so does life.

A business is a river of income flowing towards your sea of wealth.

Many streams of income reduce the risk to your business and ensure that your sea is a sea of plenty.

BRIAN MORGAN

The Core of Code 8: Many Streams of Income.

1. Many will advise you to invest in one place and watch that place as the eagle watches her nest. If that worked, it *might* make you rich; if it did not work, it would *certainly* make you poor. Do the opposite: aim to create many streams of income.

2. When others become involved in your quest for wealth, you have a responsibility to them to succeed. The greater the dependency on you, the greater your responsibility. Set a plan for any contingency; plan for many income streams.

3. Plan for the time you won't be there to keep your income streams flowing. Aim to have money working for you, rather than you working for money. Have the money work, whether you're there or not.

4. Your first income stream comes from the work you are paid to do for others. Invest at least one coin in every 10 you earn, and invest the earnings these savings make.

5. Seek additional streams by finding needs you can

fill with merchandise or services, or by bringing buyers and sellers together. Add value to everything you do and be unique, because then money will more readily flow from buyer to you.

6. The rich purchase assets that grow in value and generate income streams. These assets can be businesses, investments, services or ideas.

7. Be aware that undisciplined spending eats abundance, puts wealth out of reach, and dries up income streams.

8. Do not increase your income streams recklessly. Test each before you seek a full flow, and only move to another stream when the last is flowing freely and surely.

9. Whatever means you use to gather riches, you must follow the rules for success laid down by the ancients, or your income streams will run dry. Be aware of dangers ahead.

10. In creating streams of income, use as little of your own money as possible. Use leverage. This will lower your personal risk, and your goal should be risk-free income.

Code 9: Investments: The Magic Carpet to Riches.

Every coin you outlay is spent or invested in something, and that something goes up or down in value. Most people spend most of their coins on everyday living expenses, and, if they have anything left, spend it on things that give the appearance of wealth, like fine robes, rich carpets, fine chariots. These people may seem to be rich, but every coin they spend makes them poorer.

Avoid such spending on things that go down in value. Sacrifice. Delay your gratification until you can invest in things that grow in value, like your own home. *Gratification eats abundance.*

Investments that grow are real assets and these are the things that the rich invest in.

The rich ask questions, like: how much will this be worth 10 years from now? Do I *need* this, or do I only *want* it? The answers to these questions determine whether they will invest or not. Thus they take the sure road to riches, their Magic Carpet ride.

There may not be a perfect investment, but a perfect investment would be one that:

1. *You could sell fast.*
2. *Required no long-term management on your part.*
3. *Showed consistently high growth.*
4. *Had considerable borrowing power or ability to leverage.*
5. *Was protected from inflation.*
6. *Generated a reliable and increasing cash flow.*

Be aware that it is sometimes necessary to sacrifice high income for growth, or growth for high income.

The ability to convert an asset quickly to coin is important so that you are flexible enough to avoid coming trouble.

It has been said that the magic of compounding is the Eighth Wonder of the World - better, some say, than the Hanging Gardens of Babylon, and who can doubt it? If you reinvest the earnings from your investments, you will multiply your returns.

When you do find something that seems worthy of investment, ask yourself:

1. *Is this secure? Will my coins be safe? How safe?*
2. *When do I get the coins back that I invest? Is the timing clear and certain? Or is it the type of investment that is better left alone to gather strength, like property?*

3. *What is the return on the investment? How much can I expect to make? Can I do better elsewhere?*
4. *Can the coins I earn in this investment be reinvested to earn even more? Can I use the power of compounding?*
5. *What do I know of this investment? What do I know of the person offering it? Is that person truly an expert in this type of investment? Does he have personal experience in it?*

The objective of investing, as we learnt from the Babylonians, is to have your money earn money and the money thus earned to make more money so that eventually the stream of money from all your assets is greater than your living expenses. *When that happens, you no longer need to work.* You have found your Magic Carpet.

If you buy a house and rent it out, your objective should be to collect rent greater than the expenses it costs to run the property, including interest on debt. The same applies to any kind of investment. The income earned from it should be greater than the expenses to run it. Sometimes this is not possible, and, when this happens, the investment should only be considered if exceptional growth in value makes income sacrifice worthwhile.

When income from all streams exceeds expenses for daily living, that excess will continue to be a blessing for your family long after you are gone.

It should be a goal with each investment to earn your money back and then earn extra income for the rest of your life.

Remember: there are only two things you can do with each gold coin you take home. You can waste it or you can invest it. Your choice will make all the difference to your life.

When you buy clothing or food or a house or anything else, you are helping make someone rich. But what if you were to purchase a share of businesses that supplied such things? By becoming a part-owner of such businesses, you contribute to the profits of businesses that you part-own while making your normal purchases.

When investing in a business, consider the earning capacity of that business and at what risk it comes. Look for differences that make one business investment better than another and be prepared to change. In bad times, be prepared to go back to the essentials, like food. But any change in where you invest should be truly worthwhile. Time can be your biggest money-earner if investments are held for the long term.

If you are thinking of buying a business, look for those that have an outlook like yours, that is, those that are less interested in immediate returns than in reinvesting their earnings for growth. Understand what the company does. If its attention is consumed by greed, shun it, because it will likely take risks with your money.

Buying property is and always will be one of the best means of accumulating wealth. Some say *the* best. Buying your own home will start you on this road to riches and other properties will bring you wealth beyond dreams.

The secret to property wealth is this: buy as soon as you reasonably can, and hold it as long as you can. Wait for its value to grow. The law of supply and demand has seen to it that property has always grown in value over time, and always will.

Does not our great king understand the laws of supply and demand, and expand the walls of the city from time to time to increase the supply of land? However, despite the increase in supply, such land is usually considered attractive because all dwellings built on it will be new, so its price is high. This boosts the value of existing properties also. Thus, even an increase in supply can increase values. This is the magic of abundance. Even when Alexander arrives and others govern, land will always be made available until little is left to divide. Then shall values truly rise because demand will finally exceed supply.

Are not people moving from city to city, leaving their dwellings vacant and available for purchase? Are not the money lenders most happy to lend to those honest and hard-working citizens who wish to purchase a property for investment or build their own home? Indeed, do they not jostle one another in their efforts to help you? *If lenders scramble to invest their money in low-risk, high-profit property investment, should you not do the same?*

If you can save a reasonable portion of the purchase price, readily may you borrow for the builder and the brick-maker and the craftsmen for such a commendable purpose.

And when you and your family move into your new home, can you not repay the money lender with the same regularity you once paid the landlord? And if you have an investment property, will not the rent you collect help you pay the money lender? And will not every repayment reduce your indebtedness and increase the portion you own? Indeed, as supply decreases and demand increases, will not the value of your property grow so that you make money without lifting a finger?

Many blessings come to those who are buying their own home or investing in property. *Greatly is their cost of living decreased as time goes by.* While repayments to the money lender remain constant until the loan is fully repaid, the tenant next door will be paying increasing rent for the rest of his life. Within a few years, he will be paying more than you, and the difference will continue to grow.

But do not pay so much for your dwelling that you can never invest in other income streams. Live by the precept that the owner should be an ornament to the house, not the house to the owner, and your blessings will multiply.

Over time, property values increase, on average, by one coin per year for every 10 invested. If you invest 100 of your coins, your return would be 10 coins per year. But, if you borrowed 1000 coins from the money lender to purchase your property, your return would be 110 coins per year, which is more than the money you invested. You enjoy the earnings on what the money lender has invested in your property, and it can be more than what you had to pay him for the loan. This value growth is not money in your purse, but it *is* real wealth, and can be used to put money in your purse.

In a rental property, when this increase in value is combined with the rental you receive from tenants, *property investment becomes the envy of all and a Magic Carpet ride to riches*. This has been so in the past, and will be so as long as the sun rises in the east.

Such value growth can be put to good use, and should be, by using it as security for further borrowings for more money streams. Thus will you be following the wise adage of the Babylonians, to invest your money and to invest the earnings from that investment.

Remember, all the time that supply and demand is increasing your value, the tenants in your investment properties will be paying most of the money you have to pay the money lender. *You borrow the money, and your tenants pay it back.*

Then there comes a day when there are no more repayments to the money lender and you own your home or other property free and clear. *Ah, what a day of glory that will be, and how your family will rejoice and how they will honor you for your persistence.* For the rest of your days you will have no more to pay for rent of your dwelling, while your neighbor, who was not wise enough to purchase, will still be paying, and he will be paying more and more every year for the rest of his life, even after he can no longer work for a living. He will have a permanent commitment to the landlord and you will have an asset that grows in value every year and one that you can pass on to your children when the time comes for your final rest.

Do we not have an obligation to plan for income to continue into our old age, when we are no longer capable of working? Do we not have an obligation to provide for our family after we are gone? And will you not be honored for helping others long after you are gone?

The safest way for a person of modest means to do this is to buy a second property, and a third - until the investment is such that the future will be secure.

Investment in property is relatively safe, certain of growth over time and readily converted to coin, if necessary.

Men wise in the ways of property investment know that much of the investment is paid for by the tenants and the rest is more than paid for by growth of value as populations increase and demand exceeds supply. Someday, I hope, the king will also help by reducing taxes of the person who invests in property for the future, because such a person will not be a financial burden on the city in old age.

When buying property, remember that profit is not made only when you sell, but when you buy. When you incur debt to purchase a property, it should make sense from the day you purchase it. Property should make good financial sense whether the times be good or bad. If you pay too much to purchase, either your return on that investment will be less, or it will take longer to realize your return.

If you take on debt, be sure the debt is manageable. If you take on large debt, be sure someone else is paying for that debt.

If you develop the habit of saving and investing, you are able to take advantage when times change. When times are tough, you can buy houses and other investments with limited money. When the market improves, either you can sell those assets or gain gushing income streams from them.

If you are buying property, you must seek to *find value* or to *create value*. How can you do this?

1. *Look for people who need to sell their property because they need money. Look for sellers who are keen to sell properties because they are in trouble. To them peace of mind is more important than ownership.*
2. *Look for properties that are run down and need to be fixed. Sometimes this will allow you, when repairs are done, to greatly increase rent.*
3. *Look for properties that can be converted to another use in which higher rent can be charged. This, in turn, will increase the value of the property.*

Do not think of this as being cruel to people with problems. If you help them solve their problems in a way that does them no harm, then you can achieve your own aims while doing good to others.

Let all who read this own the roof that shelters them. Anyone determined enough can own their own home. Money lenders will gladly lend for such purposes and this money can be paid to the builder, and the brick maker and the laborer. The money lender will lend such amounts if you can demonstrate that you have saved part of the necessary money yourself and can make regular repayments on the loan. The money lender will want to see regular repayments, as regular as once you paid your landlord. Each payment will reduce the amount you owe to the money lender and, as the years pass, you will own more and more of your home. As you own more of your own home, your cost of living will reduce and more of your earnings will be available for both pleasure and more investment.

Be sure that your home is just that, a home. If it becomes more, if it becomes your palace, then it is a true liability, for it will tie up your surplus income and prevent you from growing other assets.

Investments become Magic Carpets when you follow the rules for their acquisition and stewardship, when you are patient, when you delay gratification, and when you reinvest your returns for even more profit.

Thus will the power of compounding create Magic Carpets in your life.

The Core of Code 9: The Magic Carpet to Riches.

1. Investments that grow in value are real assets. Ask yourself: what will this be worth 10 years from now? Do I *need* this, or do I only *want* it?

2. The perfect investment would be one you could sell fast, that required no long-term stewardship on your part, that showed consistently high growth, and had considerable borrowing power or ability to leverage. It should be protected from the rising cost of living and generate a reliable and increasing income stream.

3. It has been said that *the magic of compounding* is the Eighth Wonder of the World, better, some say, than the Hanging Gardens of Babylon. And who can doubt it? Do not spend the earnings from your investments, invest them and multiply your returns.

4. The objective of investing is to have your money earn money, and the money thus earned earn more money, so that eventually the stream of

money from all your assets and investments is greater than your living expenses. When this happens, *you no longer need to work.*

5. The income from an investment should be greater than all the expenses it costs to maintain that investment, including interest on debt. The only exception is where value growth is so exceptional that it makes income sacrifice worthwhile.

6. When you purchase a share in a business, consider its earning capacity and at what risk it comes. Hold for the long term, unless you have a compelling reason to change. Look for a business that has an outlook like yours. That is, one that is less interested in immediate returns than in reinvesting its earnings for growth.

7. Buying property is and always will be one of the best means of accumulating wealth. The secret to property wealth is this: *buy as soon as you reasonably can, and hold as long as you can.* Wait for its value to grow. It will.

8. Property values increase, on average, by one coin per year for every 10 invested. In a rental property, when this gain is combined with the rental you receive from tenants, property investment becomes a Magic Carpet to riches.

9. As value in property grows, the property can be used to borrow more for additional income

streams. Thus, just as you can invest additional income, you can also invest increased value, even though value is not coinage you can jingle in your purse.

10. When you finally own your dwelling free of debt, you will live rent-free for the rest of your days and have an asset that will continue to grow in value to the glory of your family.

11. When buying property, profit is not made only when you sell, but also when you buy. When you incur debt for property, it should make sense from the day you acquire it, whether the times be good or bad. Do not be swept away by excitement, pay only a fair price.

12. When buying property, seek to find value or create value. Look for sellers who have to sell, or property that is run down and can be improved. Look for properties that can be used for a different purpose and return higher rent.

Code 10: Business Secrets of the Masters

I, Tragoas, have given my testimony so that all may know my favored way to create wealth - *building businesses that can be replicated*. In following my chosen path, I have been guided by the secrets of the masters of earlier times. For the benefit of future generations, I reveal those secrets in this Code.

The secrets of the masters number seven:

1. *Find a need, and fill it. This is the primary and most necessary secret.*
2. *Develop your ideals. Love what you do, follow your destiny, seek out your purpose.*
3. *Create a vision for the future and always work towards it.*
4. *Find your own niche in a crowded marketplace.*
5. *Add value to everything you do. Everything.*
6. *In the marketplace, offer your UVP - your Unique Value Promise.*
7. *Make your business replicable, then replicate.*

There are many reasons traders fail. Some become selfish and greedy and think only of money. Some damage the world through grasping its bounty and have no regard for others. Some think only of what they can grasp now, and think nothing of the future and of those who will come after them. Some ignore the needs of people around them and think only of their own. Such ways of thinking can only lead to ruin.

Messengers inform me that Alexander is almost at our gates. I shall be brief, but I must pass on what my father taught me of the seven secrets that will surely lead to success.

\#

The first secret of the masters is to find a need and fill it.

How do you find a need?

First, look to your own life. What do you need? What would make the various aspects of your life better, easier, more enjoyable, less stressful? Think deeply and look at everything about you. Observe. Use your imagination.

Next, ask people. Ask your family, your friends, your neighbors, people in the marketplace. Is that not simplicity itself? *If you want to know what people need, ask them.*

And, if you are already in business, be sure to ask the people who chose *not* to buy from you. Find out why they did not buy.

Most traders in the marketplace find the things they wish to sell, then look for people to buy them. This is how I, Tragoas, started. However, experience has shown me that the very opposite is the most successful method. *Find buyers who are in need, and fill that need.*

Go even further. Look for people who are desperate for something, as old men in the marketplace are addicted to their opium pipes. Look for the people who really want something and will buy it at every opportunity. They make the best customers. They buy quickly and more often. And they talk to other similar people.

Find what it is that you can give your buyers that they will not get from a competitor. Find that special benefit you alone can offer and tell the world of it.

Make strong promises to your customers and be sure to keep them. If you are uncertain, it's better to promise less, and give more.

But I say, and the ancients discovered long before me, that there is something even more important than filling people's everyday needs. There are certain higher needs within the human soul that perhaps may never be expressed. The need for recognition, the need for self-confidence and self-esteem, the need for dignity, the need for love. These are just some of the higher needs of human existence.

If you can fill everyday needs, while also filling these higher human needs - needs we all feel within ourselves - then you will serve a higher purpose and be recognized for it. Then you will truly soar on the wings of an eagle, and your reputation will soar with you.

My masters reminded me that, in order for me to get money as part of my plan to become wealthy, somebody else had to give it to me. And people would only give me money if they got what they wanted in return.

Simple? Too simple? Perhaps, but not understanding this basic principle explains why many people don't make the money they want. They don't understand that people will only reward them if they can meet people's needs and desires, or relieve them of worries or fears.

The rich, let it be understood, spend a great deal of time and energy finding out what people need. And they continue to do this throughout their lives. They do not stop at the first blush of success.

All in the human family have basic needs, like food, clothing and shelter. If these basic needs are *not* met, nothing else matters. Desperation is the most powerful of motivators. But, if the basic needs *are* satisfied, people will seek to satisfy other needs.

If basic needs are met, people will turn to you if you can fill other, higher needs better than anyone else. Can you save people money or time or effort? Can you offer security, safety or comfort? Can you provide status or self-respect? In what ways can you add value to people's lives? How can you make them happier?

Find better ways to satisfy needs and these methods will become the building blocks of your success.

\#

The second secret of the masters is to develop your ideals, to love what you do, to follow your destiny, to seek out your purpose.

This is *your* life.

There are many ways to become rich, but only a limited number come from your special interests, your skills, your values.

It is true that I, Tragoas, chose many paths to riches, not only because I sought many streams of income, but because that is the kind of man I am. My interests are many. But the ancients knew that choosing business ideas that suited their own personalities created a surer path to success.

If you follow *your* dreams, you will find *your* path to success, *your* path to wealth. And if your dreams are based on the virtues and values you hold dear, even secretly in your heart, then you will find your unique way to serve mankind and please the Great God.

Use the great gift you have been given, the gift of choice. Choose well, choose wisely. *Think of what you love and you will surely love what you choose to do, and your destiny will be fulfilled.* No talent should ever be neglected.

Discovering your destiny will not always be quick or easy, but, when you do, you will have discovered who you were meant to be, how you were meant to benefit mankind. *You will have discovered your purpose for living.*

You will know when you have found it. You will sense it. It will feel right. You will feel you were born to do this.

Why *were* you born into this world? Do you ever have the feeling that you were meant to do something *important* with your life? Something *big*? Is there something missing? Could it be that you feel you should be seeking a future that will give you happiness and peace and prosperity, but one that will *truly make a difference*?

If you are thinking this way, the Codes will help you achieve what you want. But first you must be still. Let silence allow your voice within to be heard. You were taught to listen to others, but I say first listen to your own heart. There you will find your destiny.

When you are receptive in heart and mind, and only then, ideas, solutions and opportunities will flow to you.

The ancients have found that, to be truly successful, you must have a *higher purpose* when you go into business than accumulating coins. They have found that, when you have a higher purpose, magic happens and unexpected forces gather behind you to support your efforts.

I, Tragoas, have seen this happen.

Money is essential in business, but it must not be your primary objective.

Great ships seek deep water. The greatest of men think deeply to find their destiny. If you can discover yours, and live it, then shall you be fulfilled in life, and only then.

If you are still unable to discover your destiny, consider this: imagine you are at your own funeral and your best friend is rising to speak of you. What would you like that friend to say? This will tell you what you truly wish your life to become.

The ancients believed we were all born for a higher purpose. May you find yours.

#

The third secret of the masters is to create a vision for the future and always work towards it.

If you can see what will be before it becomes so, if you can imagine what your business and your life will be like in years to come, you will also be able to plan the journey to take you there.

Sit in a quiet place and assume five or 10 years have passed. What would you like to be doing? What kind of life can you imagine? What wondrous things will your business be doing? How will you be helping people? How far will you have progressed towards your destiny?

Think of where you would like to be five, 10, 20 years from now. What would you like to have achieved at the end of your working life?

The better you can hold these visions, the closer you will be to achieving them.

And the more you bring these visions to mind throughout your life, the easier it will be to overcome the negative thoughts that can ruin plans and ruin lives.

Try to foresee the obstacles you will face, but do not think of them as problems. Think of them as opportunities, for a problem solved is an opportunity gained. Do not dwell on the obstacles you foresee, dwell on the opportunities they present. In this way you will wipe out fear and doubt and replace them with self-esteem and passion for what might be.

Without a vision for the future there is no future.

The world has always needed its dreamers. Nothing would ever happen without them. Dream. See your vision. Make your plans. Do it.

#

The fourth secret of the masters it to find your own niche in a crowded marketplace.

In all streams of your business, look for the *niche* that will set you apart from all others. Finding your own niche, according to your own values, will help you select the right goods or services for *a specific group of people you can identify as needing your service*. Your own niche will help you reach such people quickly and cheaply.

It will also allow you to *bypass competition and to achieve higher profits.*

If you simply join the competition in your chosen business, as most do, you become a small fish in a big sea. You may be swallowed by the sharks. If you develop a niche, you are the only fish in your own private bay. You are protected, as long as you always seek to maintain your advantage over would-be competitors by continually increasing the value you offer.

Think of it this way: did not the kings first build a wall, and then a palace within? By seeking a niche, you build a high wall around the humble, but rich palace of your business.

A niche makes your merchandise or service easier to sell because you can concentrate on meeting the specific needs of specific buyers. Those buyers will come back to you again and again. And they will tell others of you and your fame will grow. Is not a good word from your buyers a most valuable asset? The Chinese have a proverb: "Make happy those who are near, and those who are far will come."

How do you find such a niche?

Go back to the first secret of the masters, find a need and fill it. *A niche is a section of the market that is overlooked and therefore under-serviced.*

Sometimes a niche has always been present, but not seen. Sometimes a change in people's habits or customs creates a niche. Sometimes a major upheaval, as is happening with Alexander's attack, can create a niche. Be alert and receptive. Opportunities will come to you.

Sometimes a niche can be created with new merchandise or a new service, sometimes a new way to deliver them to the marketplace, sometimes with new locations to offer them.

How will you know if you have found a niche business? There are four steps:

1. *Identify the people you wish to sell to, who they are, where they are. Is there a group that is overlooked or not yet recognized?*

2. *Discover their specific needs. Look for needs that are not being filled. What can be easier than to ask them?*
3. *Decide what goods or services would best fill those needs. Add value sufficient for them to want to buy.*
4. *Determine how, when and where to deliver these goods or services. Make it easy for them to buy.*

If each of these steps can be done, you could have a successful niche business idea.

Remember, look for people in need who have been overlooked or not satisfied. Find a way to help them. Create as much value for them as you can. This will make them want to buy, and help keep the competition away.

Find the right people. Add great value. Be unique in everything you do.

#

The fifth secret of the masters is to add value to everything you do. Everything.

This was the first lesson my father taught me. To become truly successful, you must create exceptional value, value beyond that seen in the competitive marketplace.

If your value is the same as that of everyone else, your success can be no more than theirs, and may well be less because they were there before you.

However, if you create exceptional value, you will *bypass the competition* and become a leader, rather than a follower. There are many ways to create exceptional value. Here are four of them:

1. *You can create value by improving living standards in things like better health, happier families, safer dwellings, and more work opportunities.*
2. *You can make things more convenient by offering faster service, making life simpler or easier, or by solving problems for people.*
3. *You can create more joy in the world by providing entertainment or stimulation for people on the one hand, and removing or relieving stress and worry on the other.*
4. *You can seek to fill the higher human needs by helping people achieve self-confidence, self-esteem, dignity and love.*

Go out of your way to do more for people than they expect. Walk the extra mile. Give some small thing free out of gratitude for their patronage. In a harsh, greedy world, you don't have to do much to stand out from the crowd and enjoy the gratitude of those around you. And, when you have the opportunity to do something truly worthwhile, as I did in caring for orphans, do it. Do it because it is the right thing to do and it makes you feel good. Do not do it for the reward, but the reward will come.

When people realize that you have done something for them *beyond* their expectations, that you have given value *beyond* the price charged, you have created magic just as surely as if you had called in the magicians. People will remember you and want to buy from you again and tell others.

Long will you live in the hearts of the people you serve.

\#

The sixth secret of the masters is to offer your Unique Value Promise.

Success in the marketplace is the lifeblood of business. You may have the best merchandise the world has to offer, but it means nothing if people do not know you have it, where they can buy it, how it will benefit them, and whether they can afford it.

Business *is* marketing. Marketing *is* business. By all means delegate marketing to others, but always oversee what they are doing. Your future depends on it.

Your aim in the marketplace should be:

1. *To attract more buyers.*
2. *To have each buy more.*
3. *To have each buyer return again and again.*
4. *To have buyers recommend you to others.*

To do this, you must create value for people, and you must find ways to make people aware of this value. The greater the value, the greater will be your profits. Be *unique* in the market in everything you do, and let the world know why and how you are unique. This is the essence of market success.

Remember this well: *the value of a buyer is not in what he purchases today, but in what he can purchase over a lifetime, and in what other buyers he can attract to you in that lifetime.*

Treat every buyer as if he is your friend for life. He might well be.

The most important thing is to find your unique way to break through or bypass the confusion of competition in the market. This is what will make people buy what you offer, and buy it *now*. The benefits you offer must be greater than those offered by competitors.

There are many ways to set yourself apart from the rest. You could do it with size, location, speed, ease, design, beauty, quality, effectiveness or countless others. *Search until you find what makes you gasp for breath, because it will make your buyers gasp also.*

Will your unique benefit make a difference to people's lives? Perhaps a dramatic difference? Then they will wear a path to your door.

The ancients knew many secrets of success, and perhaps none is greater than this: *that success is directly related to whether or not you are unique.* You must seek to offer merchandise and service that no-one else is offering.

When this unique offering is combined with great value for your buyers, then you are able to promise them something very special.

My Circle of Counselors called this *our Unique Value Promise - value we could promise that no-one else could.*

Our business truly soared when we adopted this as our objective and guiding principle. The Unique Value Promise compelled people to seek us out and to buy from us.

How do you find your Unique Value Promise?

You try to find what it is you can do to be unique, and you can do this best by simply asking people in the marketplace. They will tell you what they want, but cannot get.

You do not become rich by doing what everyone else does. The surest and fastest way to wealth is through your Unique Value Promise.

A Unique Value Promise is essential when competition is heavy in the marketplace. It will distinguish you from everyone else. If someone else then starts using the same Unique Value Promise, then it is no longer unique and you must find something new, some value you can add. To stay unique, to stay ahead of the herd, you must continually ask people what they want that they cannot get, and offer it. No, *promise* it.

Happy is the trader who can maintain a Unique Value Promise, because he will always attract new buyers, who will buy more and bring others to buy. And they will be happy to pay you a premium, because non-one else offers what you offer.

Let it be known that, despite the cries in the marketplace, people do not usually seek the lowest price. No, cheapest is not always best, and people know it. *What people really seek is the best value*.

And this completes the circle, because there is no better way of creating a Unique Value Promise than by always searching for better value.

#

The seventh secret of the masters is to make your business replicable, then replicate.

When you go into business, you should not just set up a business. You must set up a *system* of doing business. This is vital. It means you must understand and set up a system for marketing, for finance, for sales, for employing people, for the law, and for many other procedures that are necessary to make a business successful.

Why? The masters cite many reasons, not least of which is that *a system makes a business more likely to succeed.*

If you observe carefully, you can sometimes work with or copy from someone who has developed a successful business plan. Money lenders will lend money for such systems, because they are tested in the marketplace and found to work.

If a business owner develops a system of doing business, it will allow his wealth to grow even when he is not there, because he can teach someone else to run the business for him. He can teach them *the system*.

The objective should be to focus not on the product or service, but on the system of business, of marketing that product or service. Many people offer superior products or services, but the truly rich find a better way of marketing those products or services. They develop a system for doing this. New ideas and products and services are many, but few are the people who know how to exploit them.

If you simply own a business that you must run yourself, you are self-employed. Being self-employed means that success simply means more hard work. Having a successful business means using the benefits of other people's time. In other words, you work less but earn more.

You have skills and knowledge you wish to bring to your enterprise. Your time is valuable, because no-one else knows what is in your head. Systems allow you to pass on those skills and that knowledge to others through *repeatable processes*, so that your workers can do what you do at lower cost. This frees you to plan more systems and more success.

Now *you are being paid by the workers* who have learned your systems, and there can be many such workers once a successful pattern is established. You are also being paid for your ideas and creative thinking.

This is as it should be. Your business runs itself, and you have found freedom.

Systems are the procedures you set up within your business to ensure a predictable, repeatable result. Systems set up in all aspects of your business allow you to work *on* the business, not *in* it. They allow the business to run without you, leaving you time for thinking, for expanding, for leisure and, most important of all, for family.

And systems allow you to multiply success by replicating those systems over and over.

Let it be understood, when people look at your business, two things will determine the quality of the service you offer them:

1. *The efficiency of your systems that give them fast, convenient service.*
2. *The attitude of your workers. Buyers may forgive a poor aptitude, but never a poor attitude.*

Efficiency and *attitude* must be built into your systems. In this way, even complex things will be made simple and repeatable, and your service will be seen as great. Good systems lower costs and increase efficiency.

Let it be clearly understood: *You should do only those things that only you can do, and you should develop systems and procedures that allow others do everything else.*

Let the rule of the masters be yours: never do anything yourself when you can pay someone to do it at less cost than the money you receive for the work.

Spend your time developing systems and you will no longer be selling your time, your business will be giving you streams of income.

Even so, I, Tragoas, found that, with the help of my Circle of Counselors, I had to watch my systems and make changes when needed. I had to adapt to changing conditions. Always be aware of what is happening in the marketplace.

If you do this, you will be aware when a problem arises for the first time, and make the changes necessary to turn it into an opportunity. Thus you will master another of the success secrets of the ancients: *allow obstacles to arise only once.*

The more ways you develop to check and update your systems, the more certain you will be that you will master this secret. It is vital to determine the success factors that are critical to your systems and business, and check them closely and regularly.

I have found that the fastest way to great wealth is to build a replicable business, and then replicate it, over and over. This is the way to multiply success.

The Core of Code 10: Business Secrets of the Masters.

The first secret of the masters is to find a need and fill it. This is the core of that secret:

1. How do you find a need? Look to your own life. What would make your life better, easier, more enjoyable, less stressful? Ask others. Ask your family, friends, neighbors, people in the marketplace. If you want to know what people need, ask them.

2. Even better, look for people who want something desperately and will buy it at every opportunity. Such people buy quickly and more often, and talk to similar people.

3. Find out what you can offer buyers that they cannot get from your competitors. Find that special benefit you alone can offer, and tell the world of it.

4. Try to fulfill the higher human needs: the need for recognition, for self-confidence and self-esteem, for dignity, for love. If you can serve this higher purpose and be recognized for it, your reputation will soar.

5. If people's basic needs, like food, clothing and shelter, are not met, nothing else matters to them. Desperation is the most powerful of motivators. If basic needs *are* met, people will seek to satisfy *higher* needs. Can you save people money, time or effort? Can you offer security or comfort? Can you provide status or self-respect? Can you make people happier? How can you improve their lives?

The second secret of the masters is to develop your ideals, to love what you do, to follow your destiny, to seek out your purpose. This is the core of that secret:

1. There are many ways to become rich, but only a limited number come from your special interests, your skills, your values. Choosing business ideas that suit your own personality and character create a more certain path to success.

2. If you follow *your* dream, you will find *your* path to success, *your* path to wealth. Base your dreams on the virtues and values you hold dear, and you will find your unique way to serve mankind and please the Great God. Think of what you love, and you will surely love what you choose to do.

3. Discovering your destiny will not always be easy, but, when you do, you will have discovered your purpose for living.

4. Do you ever feel that you were meant to do something big with your life? Something that will truly make a

difference? Be still. Listen to the voice within. You will find your destiny in your own heart, in silence.

5. To be truly successful, you must have a higher purpose when you go into business than accumulating wealth. Money is essential, but it must not be your primary objective.

The third secret of the masters is to create a vision for the future and always work towards it. This is the core of that secret:

1. If you can imagine what your business and your life will be like in years to come, you will also be able to plan the journey to take you there.

2. The better you can hold your visions of the future, the closer you will be to achieving them. The more you bring your visions to mind during your lifetime, the easier it will be to overcome negative thoughts that can ruin plans and ruin lives.

3. Look ahead for obstacles, but do not think of them as problems. Think of them as opportunities, because a problem solved is an opportunity gained.

4. Without a vision for the future, there is no future. Dream. See your vision. Make your plans. Do it.

The fourth secret of the masters is to find your own niche in a crowded marketplace. This is the core of that secret:

1. Look for a niche that will set you apart from all others. Finding a niche, based on your own values, will help you select the right goods or services for a specific group of people you can identify as needing your help.

2. A niche allows you to reach specific people quickly and cheaply. It allows you to bypass competition and achieve higher profits, because you alone can fill these people's needs and they will pay you extra coins for it.

3. A niche will protect your business as long as you continually seek to maintain your advantage over your competitors. Your buyers will come back again and again, and they will tell others of you.

4. Find your niche by going back to the first secret of the masters, find a need and fill it. A niche is a section of the market that is overlooked and therefore under-serviced.

5. A change in habits or customs, or a major upheaval in people's lives can create a niche. Be alert. Opportunities will come.

The fifth secret of the masters is to add value to everything you do. This is the core of that secret:

1. To become truly successful, you must create exceptional value, value beyond that seen in the competitive marketplace. Thus will you become a leader, rather than a follower.

2. If you can offer people better health, happier families, safer dwellings, or work opportunities, you are improving their standard of living and thus creating value.

3. If you can offer faster service, or make life simpler or easier, or solve problems for people, you create greater convenience for them, and this is highly valued by all.

4. If you can provide entertainment or stimulation, or relieve stress or worry, you are creating more joy in the world. Would you not value a happy heart?

5. If you can help people achieve self-confidence, self-esteem, dignity and love in their lives, you will truly be filling their higher human needs.

6. Do more for people than they expect of you. Offer gifts, big or small, out of gratitude for their patronage. Thus will you stand out from the crowd.

The sixth secret of the masters is to offer your Unique Value Promise. This is the core of that secret:

1. Success in the marketplace is the lifeblood of business. Business *is* marketing. Marketing *is* business. Always oversee or control marketing personally. Your future depends on it.

2. Your aim in the marketplace is to attract more buyers, to have each buy more, to have each return again and again, and to have buyers recommend you to others.

3. To do this you must create value, and find ways to make people aware of this value. Be unique in everything you do, and let the world know why and how you are unique. This is the essence of marketing success.

4. The value of a buyer is not in what he purchases today, but in what he can purchase over a lifetime, and in what other buyers he can attract to you.

5. If you can find a unique way to break through or bypass the competition, this will make people buy what you offer, and buy it *now*. The benefits you offer must be greater than those offered by the competition.

6. When your unique offering is combined with exceptional value, you are able to promise buyers something special. We called this our Unique Value Promise - value we could promise that no-one else could. Our business truly soared with such promises.

7. To stay unique, to stay ahead of the herd, you must continually ask people what they want that they cannot get, and offer it. No, *promise* it.

The seventh secret of the masters is to make your business replicable, then replicate. This is the core of that secret:

1. Business masters do not set up a business, they set up a system of doing business. They set up a system for every procedure within the business. Because they give each

part of the business much thought, the business as a whole is more likely to succeed.

2. If you develop a system of doing business, your wealth can grow even when you are not there, because you can teach others to run the business for you. You can teach them the *system*.

3. Having a successful business means using the benefits of other people's time. Systems allow you to pass on your knowledge to others through repeatable processes, so that your workers can do what you do but at a lower cost. This frees you to plan more systems, and more success.

4. Systems allow you to multiply success by replicating those systems over and over. This is leveraging success.

5. You should do only those things only you can do, and you should develop systems and procedures that allow others to do everything else.

6. Watch your systems and make changes when needed. Thus will you be aware when a problem arises for the first time, and make the change necessary to turn it into an opportunity. Allow obstacles to arise only once.

BRIAN MORGAN

Code 11:
The Special Few.

Many are those who appear to be about to plunge into wealth, and have all they need to do so. But they don't take that final step. They don't act.

Perhaps they feel unworthy. Perhaps they are, deep within, afraid of failure, or of what changes success will bring.

Let such people read these Codes and find the courage to do what is necessary. If they do not act, they will not succeed. As a sage once said: *better to try and fail, than to fail to try.*

If you have a wealth-creating idea and a burning desire to have that wealth and you take fearless action to achieve it, nothing can stop you. Everything else you need can be borrowed or bought. You can assemble the people who have the experience, the money, the skills and the other resources that you lack. All of these people are waiting for someone to say, "Follow me".

You are free to think for yourself. Freedom of thought is our primary freedom. It's the last freedom we lose under oppression. It's the freedom we must prize most. It is essential to the inherent dignity and worth of every member of the human family.

We are endowed by the Great God with reason and conscience. We must use them to achieve our destiny.

To achieve anything in life, your goal must be clearly established in your mind. When the goal is clear, the steps to achieving it will also become clear.

But the most important thing is the kind of person you are *before* you established your dreams, or the kind of person *you believe you can become*. You must have the character and the attitude and the willpower and the determination to achieve your aim, otherwise the things you need to do will never get done.

Your true value lies not in what you have, nor even in what you do, but in what you *are*. If value is in *you*, value will come to your purse. Fortune is something that must be won; honor is something that must not be lost.

The sage Plato once said, "There are three classes of people: lovers of wisdom, lovers of honor, lovers of gain." I say to you, why not strive for all three?

The Great God has given you two great gifts: time and choice. It is up to you to do what you will with both.

Sometimes we wonder if we should change our lives. I, Tragoas, say to you that we *do* change our lives - every day, countless times. We change our lives when we chose one task over another, one dwelling over another, one friend over another. We change when we decide to have a baby, take a journey, put off a task or do it, stay in bed or get up, rest or work, smile or curse, play with children or ignore them.

No, my friends, the question is not *whether* we should change our lives. We do it every day. The question is: *how* should we change our lives?

With each gold daric that enters your purse, you can determine your future. Spend it on foolish things and you will be poor. Spend it on acquiring assets and you will be rich. The choice is yours. *Every day you make decisions to either be rich or poor.* If you choose to be rich, share this knowledge with your children and loved ones to prepare them for their future. Your future and that of your family will be determined by your choices now. Let others light their candle at your wisdom.

The ancients have told us that we do not inherit this world from them, we borrow it from our children. *It is our obligation to leave this world better than we found it for our children's sake.*

Of those who read these words, some will not be able to understand or to imagine a life of riches.

Some will not believe that a rich man would show the way to true riches to others. But there will be some with a dance in their step and a new enthusiasm for they will see a way to a brighter future. They will see a new world of riches and they will see a great opportunity.

There will be those who will laugh at what they read because of its simplicity. But are not truth and beauty always simple?

In truth, many will hear these words.

Some will listen.

Few will act. The special few.

The Great God has already smiled on future generations and, through these Codes, this wisdom from the ancients gives them the means to become part of the few.

The God has given freely of the gift that is beyond all others - the gift that makes all things possible to those who would achieve them. The gift that makes other gifts, like the gift of courage, the gift of strength and the gift of love, possible.

Yes, the God has smiled upon many, and upon you, and given you the greatest gift of all, *the gift of choice*.

Given the choice between gold and wisdom, which would you choose? Most men spend the gold and ignore the wisdom and end up with neither.

Use wisdom to make the right choices every day. These are the choices that will give you the kind of memories that will sustain you in your old age. These are the choices that will ensure you have few regrets when the time comes to greet the Great God.

Remember that many people do not become happy with more money. Greed is never a recipe for happiness. Real happiness comes from looking for values that are more important to us than our money. *Self worth is more important than net worth*. But is there any reason you should not seek to improve both?

Is it possible to change your attitude and so change your life? Is it possible to progress from a state of misery to a state of inner peace and excellence? The ancients say it is - and it is simple. All you must do is act as if you were already the kind of person you wish to be. If you continue to act so, you will be so.

The ancients have long said that mediocre people who take persistent action to improve their lives go further than superior people who do not.

The character of a person is the arbiter of his fortune.

#

Alexander is at the gates of Persepolis and I have no time for stories, and yet I must tell what happened not long ago, when the Macedonian met the Greek sage Diogenes.

This Diogenes was the one who said that he has the most who is content with the least. He gave away all his possessions except his drinking bowl, and he even gave that away when he saw a slave boy drinking water from cupped hands.

Alexander came to him to offer his respects and to receive wise counsel. They talked much.

Finally, Diogenes asked him what his plans were. The Macedonian said he planned to conquer all of Greece. And then? asked Diogenes. Alexander said he planned to conquer all of Asia Minor. And then? asked Diogenes. The Macedonian king said he then planned to conquer the world. And then? asked Diogenes. After that, said Alexander, he planned to pursue the leisure arts and enjoy life. Diogenes was thoughtful. Why not save yourself all that trouble, he said, and enjoy life now?

The Macedonian who now bears down on Persepolis did not listen to the counsel. But the advice is there for those wise enough to accept it. Mark my words: Alexander, who is not satisfied with the whole world, will one day, like all of us, have to settle for a tomb.

Is it not a pity that the man they call Alexander the Great does not know what we know - that you do not have to conquer the world to claim all you want of its wonders and abundance?

There need be no conflict between accumulating riches and enjoying life along the way. Indeed, there should be no such conflict. The destination may or may not be reached - the Great God will have a say in that - but the journey is there to enjoy.

All of us have much to offer the world, and the world has an abundance to offer in return. Great are the riches in that abundance. We must each develop the person we are, then the plan of what we shall offer the world and how we shall offer it. Deploy our talents into the world for the benefit of others and our rewards will be great.

One of the great compensations and ironies of this life is that no one can give to others without receiving in return.

The more we give, the more we get.

May the Great God smile upon you.

BRIAN MORGAN

The Core of Code 11: The Special Few.

1. If you do not act, you will not succeed. If you have a wealth-creating idea and a burning desire to have that wealth, and you take action to achieve it despite your fear, nothing can stop you.

2. Freedom to think for yourself is your primary freedom. It is essential to your inherent dignity and worth as a human being. You are endowed with reason and conscience. You must use them to achieve your destiny.

3. True value lies not in what you have, nor even in what you do, but in what you *are*. If value is in *you*, value will come to your purse. Fortune is something that must be won; honor is something that must not be lost.

4. You have two great gifts, time and choice. It is up to you what you will do with both. Every day you make decisions to be either rich or poor. With every gold daric that enters your purse, you can determine your future. Spend them on foolish

things, and you will be poor. Use them in the ways of the ancients, and you will be rich.

5. The question is not *whether* you should change your life. You do it every day. The question is *how* should you change your life?

6. Greed is never a recipe for happiness. Self worth is more important than net worth. But why not seek to improve both? Your own character is the arbiter of your fortune.

7. There need be no conflict between accumulating riches and enjoying life along the way. We all have much to offer the world, and the world offers abundance in return. Deploy your talents into the world for the benefit of others and your rewards will be great.

8. May the Great God shower you with blessings.

Epilogue

Tragoas ended his dictation to the scribes with an appeal to his Great God for us, the future generations he was never sure he could reach. We are left to wonder what his God had in store for him when the Macedonian arrived. Did he live? Did he have time to flee? We can but hope.

Ironically, his words reached us because of a torch held by a drunken Alexander, the man he despised for his greed. A torch and a drunken rage started a blaze that baked the clay tablets and preserved them from the ravages of time.

Could it be that an old man's words might yet set a torch under the bonfire of greed that has consumed much of the world, just as Tragoas feared? Is it possible that the world might see that the way to real wealth lies not in the clutching hands of greed, but in the abundance we can all create and we can all share?

The thoughts of many ancients combined to make this legacy from Tragoas. But those thoughts will be wasted unless one person acts on them. You.

You could, like many, die wondering, or you could purchase the future of your dreams by your action today. Begin. Take one step.

A journey is not made up of giant leaps; it's made one step at a time. The only step any of us have to take right now is the next one. Never be afraid that the journey might be slow. That which grows slowly strikes deep roots.

Forgive this plea on behalf of Tragoas, but this world could be better, could it not?

What can you do, what are you willing to do to make it so? Are you discontented? Man's best achievements spring from discontent.

Unless we are prepared to eat each other like sharks, we must accept that attitudes in this world need reform. All reforms start with personal opinions and individual actions. If the opinions are true, if the actions inspirational, others will follow. A quiet revolution is a revolution still.

The world needs change, but each of us cannot do it alone. All we can do, as Tragoas suggested, is change ourselves, and hope others follow.

So, this book comes down to a single decision we each have to make alone. We have to decide whether his tablets are worthless lumps of baked clay, or whether they are the bricks upon which we can build our future.

Throw this book down, and you have made a decision. Make notes, dog-ear, underline, and you've made another. That's the choice.

It's not every author that wants his book mutilated like that, but this one does.

May the spirit of Tragoas live, and long may you prosper in that spirit.

###

BRIAN MORGAN

Your Notes

THE RICHEST MAN IN PERSIA

Your Notes

BRIAN MORGAN

Your Notes

About the author

Brian Morgan is a former business leader and a national award-winning journalist, editor and author. He lives with his wife, Judy, and members of his family on the Central Coast of NSW, Australia, after living most of their lifetime in Sydney.

Brian received a private education through high school and studied business, accounting and other tertiary courses, including applied psychology, media law, computer programming and IT, marketing and creative thinking through technical colleges, correspondence college and specialist colleges. He studied creative writing and journalism through correspondence college.

Since then, he has taught at TAFE colleges, served as a business seminar leader and conducted workshops for and lectured to various business and community groups.

Brian was the founder of a number of businesses and institutions set up for charitable, educational and business purposes. He has had not one, but three successful careers, and has now embarked on a fourth.

More details are available on his website, but he has chalked up a number of major achievements in national and multi-national companies. As an employee or as a consultant, he has experience in many industries and also event organization and management.

He founded the Australian Institute for the Self-employed to educate and train the self-employed and small business people, and he has written a Small Business Course studied by thousands of people around Australia.

He has served as editor, editor-in-chief, manager and publisher on a range of mastheads in Australia, winning numerous state and national awards in the process. His writing has been translated for Chinese, Vietnamese and Japanese audiences. He has published five of his own national magazines, including three business magazines, and has appeared on best-seller lists in the US and UK.

Brian Morgan has given many years of service to his community and to a variety of business and charitable organizations in Australia, but has always declared his family to be his first and foremost interest.

Visit www.BrianMorganBooks.com for more detail.

www.ingramcontent.com/pod-product-compliance
Lightning Source LLC
Chambersburg PA
CBHW030934180526
45163CB00002B/561